The Retirement Umbrella

The Retirement Umbrella

Protect Your Standard of
Living and Enjoy Peace of
Mind in Retirement

Kevin Bard

Table of Contents

Introduction.
Suitable or Not?

Every day, you make decisions: big decisions, small decisions, and every kind in between. You make choices about what's suitable for you. Some of the biggest decisions you'll ever make are about your retirement years, and everywhere you look, there's plenty of conflicting advice to be had. So when it comes to making those choices, how do you know what's right for you?

Let me tell you a story. One thing you should know about me is that I'm a country boy at heart. So in late 2006, my wife and I moved out to the country with our kids. We found this old farm house that had been refurbished. It had been decorated to 1800s' standards. In fact, the person who built the house bought it from the original owners of the land that established the property in 1826. There are old barns on the property that are well over a hundred years old. I'm not sure when the house was originally built, but the owners added a new section onto it back in the mid-'90s and made it look like a very old farm house.

The Retirement Umbrella

We wanted to change a couple of things when we moved in, but neither my wife nor I are very good at decorating. We like certain things. When I walk into somebody's room, I can tell you what I think looks nice, but walking into a room and saying, "Maybe we should put this color here, or that color here, or these drapes, or those floor coverings," we're no good at that.

We decided that we needed help to decorate the living room, so we decided to hire an interior decorator who had incredible taste. I looked at some of her work—she did tremendous, beautiful rooms and decorations—and we really liked her style, so we asked her to come over. When she came to our house and walked into our living room, she saw that we have this big, beautiful stone fireplace that goes all the way up to the ceiling. It's probably close to 20 feet tall. She immediately said, "That's the focal point of the room, and we're going to decorate to that." I said, "All right." That sounded good to me.

Now I knew how I wanted to use the room. My boys and I, we love to play and wrestle. We love to have our little ninja sword fights—I like to train my young Jedi apprentices in the living room. We use this room for family get-togethers, watching TV, watching movies together, and wrestling, and all those sorts of things. We live in that room. We don't want a showplace.

Introduction. Suitable or Not?

Then the decorator started to come up with a lot of different ideas. One of them was, "Let's get the TV out of here. Let's put it in a different room. We're going to use this room for more of a showplace." She had furniture in mind that didn't meet the needs that I had in mind. I wanted furniture that we didn't have to worry about sitting on or playing on. We're not going to tear the furniture apart, but I don't want to be ultra-cautious about even sitting on it. She had these ideas of what she wanted to do. I kept telling her, "This is a room that we enjoy as a family. This is the room that my boys and I wrestle in. If we move the TV out, and we just use this as a showplace, then where are we going to do those things, and what will we use this room for?" She said, "This room will be for when you have guests over." That didn't sit well with me, because I felt that we'd be wasting the space.

I went along with some of her ideas, but we ended up having to compromise. She compromised on the style that she had in mind. This vision that she had was a beautiful room that would be the focal point, the showplace of the house, but her vision didn't fit my need. It didn't fit the needs of our family. It certainly would have been beautiful if we'd let her just do it, but it wasn't what we wanted. It wasn't what we needed. We both had to compromise, and we ended up with a room that was really nowhere near what I had envisioned it to be, and nowhere near what she had envisioned. It certainly came out nice, but it wasn't what either one of us wanted.

The bottom line is this: When she did her analysis of the room, and proposed decorating it, she came up with a plan that was suitable for **her** vision. What she didn't do was come up with a plan that was what **we** wanted, or what we needed. That is the difference between what I call the **suitability standard**, and the needs-based standard, or what we know in my industry as **fiduciary standards**.

I'm a fiduciary, and that means my concerns are the needs of my clients, not necessarily what's suitable for them based on their particular answers to some standard questions. I'm not going to say to them, "Well, that's suitable based on your age. That's suitable based on how much time you have before you need these monies." I'm going to ask other questions of my clients. I'll ask, "What are your needs? Will you need income? When will you need income? How will you be pulling your income? Where are you going to get that income? How will taxes affect your income? How will all of these things tie together?" These determine the client's real needs. Investment strategies based on fiduciary standards, or the needs of the client, will often be completely different from investment strategies based on what we call suitability standards.

Introduction. Suitable or Not?

I like to consider myself as not just a fiduciary, but as someone who helps other people make good, sound decisions based on facts—not on myths, misconceptions, or emotions. All too often people make their decisions based on emotion. They ignore the facts. They heard this; they heard that. Maybe somebody on the TV says something that gets them all excited, but they don't dig any further to look at the facts. I can tell you this for certain: It's never a good idea to bet your future standard of living on an emotion. Think back: How many times in your life have you made emotional decisions? We've all done it. Maybe you've done things, or said things, or reacted in a certain way because of anger, fear, or some other emotion, but you know it wasn't really the best reaction you could have had. We're all guilty of that. What we're trying to do in investment planning is make sure that we take the emotion out of it. We want to help people make good, sound decisions based on facts.

We live in a new, rapidly changing world, and we don't want to use old world methods or old world thinking. When I was in high school—okay, a few years back—the video game Pong was popular. Now it's kind of funny. When I show my kids Pong, they just laugh. "Are you kidding me? This is it? This is a video game?" When I was their age, we were all excited about it. Now it's old school. Another one of those old school games was Atari. Remember that?

The Atari was the latest and greatest. It was the hot video game. Where's Atari today? The problem with those two games is they simply didn't keep up with the changes that were happening in the gaming industry. The companies were guilty of what I call old world thinking. Now they're gone. I find that all too often, people are also guilty of old world thinking. They make decisions based on how things used to be. In this new world, in the new society that we live in, we have to keep up with what's happening now, and not just in the marketplace.

Investment planning, for example, is completely different today than it was in the '90s. It has to be, because in the '90s the market took off like a rocket. The market went up and it didn't seem like it would ever come back down. People had a feeling of euphoria, as if they'd never have to worry about money again, and they could retire at 50. Well, we saw what happened. A lot of the factors that drove the market to all-time highs in the '90s were actually problems that caused the crashes of the 2000s.

Different times call for different strategies. We have to change with the times, but we also have to use strategies that fit our needs—and not just current needs, but also our future needs going forward into retirement. It's a completely different type of plan than when we're trying to grow money. When we're growing money, we look at taking more risks and trying to get a bigger return. When we're in retirement, taking a bigger risk and trying to get a bigger return can be a massive mistake, especially when we're drawing income from our investments. Again, we want to keep up with the new world thinking: design the plan based on our current needs, and adjust it so that as we continue on, it will meet our future needs as well.

Too often I find that people have an investment strategy based on what their advisor thought their growth should be, and it's a strategy that does not meet their real needs. This is what I ask my clients: **Is it more important for your money to grow, or for it not to shrink?**

When we look at the difference between suitability standards and fiduciary standards, it always goes back to the needs of the client. I don't care what products, or tools, or vehicles that we use for investment. This is what I care about: How does this fit the needs of my clients? We need to get away from just putting people into investments that are suitable based on their age, or risk tolerance, or time frame. What we need to ask instead is: What do we want this money to do, what do we need it to do, and how will we accomplish that?

One of the factors that we always have to consider is where you are going to get your income when you retire. I'll address this in more detail further on in the book, but basically there are four sources from which we are going to be drawing income in retirement.

The first is Social Security. The second is a pension, if you have one. Next is income from continuing to work in retirement (full-time, part-time, consulting, etc.), and last is your own savings and investments. If you don't want to work anymore once you retire, you're down to three sources. If you don't receive a pension and you don't want to work, you're down to two sources—your savings and investments, and Social Security. Will those be enough to meet your current or future standard of living, and for how long? That is the key thing to consider. Where are you going to get your income? How much will you need to meet your standard of living? Where is any shortfall going to come from? Your retirement plan needs to answer these questions. This book will help you look closely at them and develop a plan that meets your needs.

Chapter 1.
The #1 Fear in Retirement

When I first entered this business full-time in 1993, the strategies I was creating for people were completely different from what they are today. Back then, it was all about trying to grow their money. As I started to meet more and more with older people, especially the senior seniors—anybody who has been in retirement 10 years or more, I call senior seniors— I saw that their needs were different.

The fastest growing segment of our population is age 65 and up. By 2030, according to the U.S. Census Bureau, one in five Americans will be over age 65. By 2060, that group will grow to include one in four Americans. [1]

People are living longer. We all know people who are living well into their 80s and 90s. That means they are also living more years in retirement. In all of my seminars, I ask people to rate their fears in retirement. The number one concern is always the fear of running out of money.

It's often said that the number one fear for most people is speaking in public. But I can tell you that every time I ask people what their number one fear is, I hear, "Running out of money before I run out of life." I meet people all the time who come to me from fear of running out of money. Their underlying question is: will my money last as long as I do?

We all have these fears—some founded, some not—and nothing illustrates these retirement fears better than a story.

A Tale of Two Couples

Some years ago, I went to a client's home. It was the middle of winter and we'd just had a snow storm up in Michigan. When I got to the house, I saw an older gentleman—I'll call him Walter—out in the driveway shoveling snow by hand. He was in his mid-80s. As you can imagine, he was working very hard; shoveling snow is no easy task. When Walter saw me, he said, "I'll be right with you, just go on in," and talking and coughing, he added, "have a seat and I'll be right in."

I went inside and saw that it was a tastefully, modestly decorated home. The house was small but in very good shape. Everything the couple had—all their furniture, their carpet, even their car—was older but in very good shape. Their car was probably

Chapter 1. The #1 Fear in Retirement

15 years old. It was obvious that they didn't spend a lot of money.

When I sat at the table and started talking to Walter's wife—let's call her Ilse—she started to tell me their story. They had come from Germany when they were very young. They had lost everything in Germany when the Nazis came to power. When they got to the United States, they just started working and they worked and they worked.

After I'd been speaking with Ilse for a few minutes, Walter came in. He said, "Give me a minute here." He lay down on the couch, and he was breathing so heavily I was afraid he was going to have a heart attack.

Once he had rested for a few minutes, he came into the dining room, sat down at the table with Ilse and me, and started talking. Walter told me that they had saved every dime that they could get. They had worked all the overtime that they could possibly work. They made their own lunches. They never went on vacation. They would go to work and then go home. They never even went out to dinner. They were always very frugal in their spending.

When I did a complete analysis with them, I discovered that they had almost $3 million in various banks. When I asked them what their number one fear was, they said running out of money. I was shocked. They had almost $3 million! They had large pensions and they had Social Security income. Between those two sources of income, they were not only meeting all of their regular obligations, they were actually saving money. They weren't touching their accumulated savings at all. They were saving even more on top of it.

I couldn't understand why they would fear running out of money. But they were afraid that they would get sick, maybe have to go into a nursing home, and that the cost of nursing home care would just wipe them out. That's certainly a common fear, and something that we all have to consider. Long-term care can take a huge bite out of our hard-earned savings, and we'll take a closer look at that later in this book. But in Walter and Ilse's case, their fear was unfounded because of the amount of income that they were receiving from Social Security and pensions.

If Walter and Ilse had drawn even a very small percentage from their portfolio, it probably would have easily provided them enough income to take care of nursing care expenses without really dipping into any other savings. Why were they so afraid? There was no question of passing their money on; they had no children or family who would inherit. But it was emotional for them. They had deep fears that had built up throughout their entire lives, going all the way back to when they were young and their

Chapter 1. The #1 Fear in Retirement

families lost everything in Germany. They lived in fear of that happening again.

I often cite Walter and Ilse as an example of what I consider to be an unfounded fear. In all likelihood, Walter and Ilse will never have to worry about outliving their money.

Now let's talk about the other side of the coin. I also see people who are not even thinking about retirement or thinking about how long their money will last even as they start to retire.

I recently met with a younger couple. We'll call them Gary and Julie. They're both in their mid-50s. They decided to retire early, knowing they were going to get a pension. They decided to turn on their retirement assets early—we'll talk about the pitfalls of doing that later in the book—and as they started to draw money from their retirement savings, they didn't stop to consider how long these retirement savings would last. They thought that they had plenty of money in the account and running out wasn't even an afterthought. They felt that their pensions and their savings would be enough to sustain them in retirement with no problem. They had no fear of running out of money.

But Gary and Julie should have been afraid. Based on how much they were drawing from their savings and investments, I calculated that unless they stopped drawing what they were drawing out, they were going to run out of money before they were 70 years old. Then they would be completely broke. The only thing they would have left to live on would be Social Security and pensions, and those would not be enough to sustain their current standard of living. They had what I call unrealistic expectations.

In both of these cases, we see couples who haven't thought things through logically. They've made decisions emotionally. Walter and Ilse made a decision to live extremely frugally, to not even enjoy the fruits of their labors in any way. They didn't even go out to dinner because they were so afraid that they would run out of money. That's an unfounded fear because they have saved more than enough for their projected needs. There's no need for them to worry about it. Gary and Julie, on the other hand, absolutely should be worried because they spend more than they're bringing in. At some point they're not going to have any money left, but they were not at all concerned because they thought that they had plenty. They had never really looked at the reality.

When we sat down with Gary and Julie and started pointing out some numbers, their eyes were opened and they finally became concerned—but before then? Nothing. They were not at all worried. Why is that? Well, they had also made a decision emotionally. They had made their retirement decision based on what they wanted to do, not on the facts of their situation. They based their decisions on emotion. What I like to do, and what I did for Gary and Julie, is help people better understand the facts that are involved in their retirement planning. Where are they going to get their income? What's the realistic expectation of how long their money will last?

I'm not trying to be mean, but I do want to be realistic. We can't get a 10 percent return on our money while we're drawing income from that money without taking a lot of stock market risk. Remember, a loss will take a *huge* bite out of your investments very quickly. What's the realistic outlook of how long your money will last? What are you actually spending per month and where are you going to get that money?

I sat down with Gary and Julie and we went through how much income they would need each month to meet their obligations and maintain their standard of living. When we do that we look at everything: your basic living expenses, your house, your utilities, your car, any miscellaneous expenses, entertainment expenses like golf, eating out, and maybe some travel. Think about how expensive those things can be. Where are you going to get the money for those expenses? In Gary and Julie's case, we were dealing with unrealistic expectations. They should have had a fear of running out of money, but they didn't because they had never thought it all the way through.

No one had ever walked them through the process of assessing how much money they would really need in retirement, where they would get it from, and how long their money would last. When I did that with them, things changed dramatically. They finally understood that based on how much money they were pulling out of their portfolio, they were going to be broke and completely out of savings before they even turned 70. I calculated that they would run out of money in their late 60s. Gary and Julie's expectations about their retirement years were just as unrealistic as Walter and Ilse's, but in an entirely different way.

What Do *You* Expect from Retirement?

The next time you're at your supermarket, your church, your local department store, take a good look around. You will see a lot of older people, most of them retired. Are your retirement expectations realistic? You've got to look at the facts to properly prepare for retirement so that you can maintain the standard of living that you want in your retirement years.

We know that people are living longer. Think about how many people you know who are 90 years old, or even older. For a married couple, both in good health, the probability that at least one of them will

Chapter 1. The #1 Fear in Retirement

live into their 90s is quite high. How long will your retirement years last? Will your money last as long as you do?

What is your current standard of living? You need to calculate what your costs are. What do you want to do in your retirement? What will that cost? If your plan when you retire is to sit on the front porch and rock, that's pretty cheap. You don't have to have a lot of money to maintain that lifestyle. But what if you're not ready to do that yet? What if you want to do a little traveling, or spend some time with the grandkids and enjoy life? That's going to cost a little more than buying a rocking chair and a blanket. Add to that the various risk that can require additional income to overcome and you have the potential for running out of money before you run out of life.

I used to open up all my workshops with this story; I first heard it many years ago.

There was a wealthy man who built himself a gargantuan Olympic-sized swimming pool in his yard. He had it custom-made to his personal specifications. It was the most incredible pool that you could imagine, right there in his yard. He had an electronic cover installed on the pool, so he could open and close it with just the touch of a button. Once the pool was all finished and filled with water, he closed it up and decided he was going to have a grand pool opening party. He invited all of his friends, his relatives, and his neighbors; he had a string quartet playing; he had caterers serving hors d'oeuvres and drinks. It was a first class party and everybody was having a grand time.

When the party was well underway, the wealthy man went to the microphone to make an announcement. He asked everyone to gather around the pool. So all the party-goers clustered around the pool, eager to see the grand unveiling. The wealthy man said, "Before I unveil the pool, I'm going to make an offer to all of the young single men in the audience here. If one of you is brave enough to just jump right into this pool after it's uncovered, and swim all the way to the other side, I will give you your choice of one half of my wealth or my beautiful daughter's hand in marriage."

The crowd buzzed in anticipation, and the young men all moved close, each eager to be the first into the pool as soon as it was unveiled. The wealthy man hit the button, the cover came back to reveal the pool, and . . . not a soul jumped into the pool. Instead everyone gasped and jumped back. Why? Because in the pool were seven of the biggest, nastiest, hungriest alligators you could ever imagine. The alligators were fighting and snapping, just waiting for a meal. And the wealthy man looked at the young men and said, "Well, on your mark, get set, go." But not one man jumped in that pool. Not one single man took

Chapter 1. The #1 Fear in Retirement

him up on his offer. He just said, "Well, I'm disappointed, but I understand. Start up the band, pass those hors d'oeuvres, and let's just continue on with the party."

The band began to play, and the waiters started serving again, when suddenly there was a splash. Everyone quickly turned just in time to see a young man in the pool, swimming for his life. He was swimming, kicking away the alligators, pushing and shoving, and finally he got all the way to the other side. He pulled himself out of the pool, huffing and puffing. Everyone started cheering and clapping; they couldn't believe he had actually done it. The wealthy man was thrilled. He walked up to the young man and said, "That was incredible, my young friend. I am a man of my word, so you now have your choice: one half of all my wealth or my beautiful daughter's hand in marriage, whichever you decide."

The young man looked at him and replied, "I'm sorry, but I don't want to marry your daughter and I don't want any of your wealth. All I want is the name of the sucker who pushed me in the pool."

I like that story because I think the alligators are a great analogy for the unexpected dangers in life, the things that happen when we least expect them. Who would have ever expected the alligators in the pool, ready to take a bite out of the first person to hit the water?

The Retirement Umbrella

When it comes to retirement, it's not alligators we're worried about. There are dangers that can take a bite out of your retirement income, but they are dangers that we can anticipate and plan for.

In this chapter, we've been talking about retirement fears—those that are founded and those that are not. For many people, the fear of running out of money really is a legitimate fear. There are factors that actually can take a big bite out of our hard-earned retirement savings. They include taxes, inflation, stock market risk, interest rate fluctuations, health care costs, long-term care needs, probate, estate planning, and longevity risk. We'll take a closer look at these later in the book, but for now I want to point out that one of the biggest factors is one we can control: procrastination. It is that very human tendency to put off till tomorrow what could (and usually should) be done today. How often do we manage to convince ourselves that there will be plenty of time later to make sound financial decisions? Taking action now and not putting it off can go a long way toward protecting your retirement savings.

You've already taken a step towards overcoming retirement procrastination: You're reading this book.

And the good news is that by overcoming procrastination, by looking at the facts, and by doing some careful planning, you can protect yourself against the factors that can erode your retirement savings. You can set up a **retirement umbrella** that will protect your hard-earned money from financial storms.

Wouldn't it be great to be able to let go of the fear of outliving your money? Wouldn't it be great to simply look forward to living the retirement you've always dreamed of?

The Retirement Umbrella

Chapter 2.
Your Retirement Dream

We've all seen the video from that day back in 1963: Martin Luther King Jr., standing on the steps of the Lincoln Memorial, looking out at the thousands of people gathered on the National Mall and telling them, "I have a dream...." It's such a powerful message. The words touch us all.

You have a dream too. We all do. We dream that one day we'll be able to stop working and enjoy the fruits of our hard-earned labor. My dream is that together we can make that happen.

Right now if you are still working, it's still just a dream. It hasn't come true yet, but with proper planning we can make that dream come true. And I'll tell you honestly: if you don't make a plan, you risk that dream turning into a nightmare. Remember that the number one fear is running out of money, outliving your money. What happens then? You're going to be in retirement a long, long time. Many people will be in retirement 30-plus years. You probably know people who have been in retirement that long. As of the writing of this book, my mother is 92 years old. She's been in retirement for many years, and she's in very good health. She's going to be in retirement even longer. You don't want to risk outliving your money.

I've worked with a lot of different people who are enjoying their retirement and have been in retirement a long time. They're living their retirement dreams with no worries of outliving their money, because of the type of planning that we've done with them. We've made sure that they don't have to worry about where they're going to get their income. They have money that's coming to them on a regular basis without ever having to worry about what's happening with the stock markets, bond markets, interest rates, or inflation.

As I write this book, I'm 56 years old. When I retire I want to be able to slow down. I don't think I'll ever say, "That's it for me." I love my job so much that I'll continue to work on a part-time basis, just because I enjoy the work. Of course, I work 70-plus hours a week now and I definitely won't work that many hours when I retire. I'll be slowing way down. I'll be doing it more to just visit clients and enjoy the time that I can spend with different people, not to worry about growing my business.

My dream in retirement is that my wife and I will be able to just travel around in a motor home. Right now, we love to camp. I want to continue to do that. I want to do that with the grandkids. I want to be able to see places like the Grand Tetons again, and enjoy the beautiful countryside out there. I want to hike in Yosemite. I want to see the Sequoia National Forrest. I want to be able to bring my grandkids there. I want to be able to do things like that without having to worry about the obligations of daily work. That's my dream. I'm planning to use my retirement years, while I'm healthy, to see some of the different places in this country that we're blessed to have.

Making Your Retirement Dream a Reality

How do I plan to make my retirement dream come true?

First of all, I am not betting my future standard of living, or my retirement dream, on the stock market. I'm not going to count on the stock market to provide my wife and me with the income that we need to sustain our standard of living for the rest of our lives. That's way too risky. I'm certainly going to be invested in the stock markets, but what I do is invest money into the stock market in amounts that really won't affect my future standard of living. For lack of a better term, it's money that I play with. I buy certain stocks, mutual funds, and exchange-traded funds, in a brokerage account. I look at it every few months. Every once in a while, I'll go into the account, make some trades, and move stuff around a little bit.

I don't like losing money, but I know for certain that if I do lose something in one of these assets, if one of those stocks does very poorly, it is not going to affect my standard of living in the least. If the account goes up, that's great. If it goes down, that's unfortunate, but it won't affect my standard of living. This is what I suggest to all my clients: **You can be in the market as much as you want, but don't let it affect your future standard of living.** Don't count on it to be the sole support for your future income. Don't count on it to be the source that you're going to be pulling income from. Why? Because the market will break your heart more than it will ever help you. Remember the question I asked earlier: **Is it more important for your money to grow, or for it not to shrink?** Is it more important for you to get a 30 percent return or avoid a 30 percent loss?

If you are in retirement or close to retirement, and you're in the stock market, I challenge you to think long and hard about that question. Do you really need as much of a return as you're risking your money to try to get? In many cases, you will find that the returns that you're getting are nowhere near what you think they are. We're going to address that one in more detail in Chapter 4.

Chapter 2. Your Retirement Dream

I met a gentleman the other day, a new client. We'll call him Joe. He's 52 years old, and he hopes to retire at age 65, so he has some time to plan. Joe has taken some huge hits in the market over the last 10 years, and he realizes that he can't afford to keep doing that and expect that the money he has accumulated will provide him with the retirement income that he's going to need. We took a look at how much he had saved, and how much of that he's probably going to have to pull from in retirement. When we did that, we could see that the rate of return he needed to sustain his future retirement plan was really only about five percent. He doesn't need to take all kinds of risk to get a five percent return. I suggested that we take some of his money and put it into safer strategies that would be much lower risk, even some guaranteed strategies that go up when the market goes up but don't go down when the market goes down.

Joe realizes that he's got quite a bit of money saved. Now it's not about how much more he needs to save. Now he just has to protect what he has, by not taking so much risk with it. He's been taking more risk than he needs to take. Joe doesn't need to get a 30 percent return. He doesn't even need to get a 12 percent return on that money. If he gets a five to seven percent return, he will continue to grow his money, keep up with inflation, and still have plenty of money to draw income from to maintain his standard of living in retirement. He has plenty of time to continue to buy into the market, as long as he protects the assets he doesn't need to risk. Joe can look forward to maintaining his standard of living and making his retirement dream come true.

When we talk about planning for your retirement dream, we look not only at savings, but also at every aspect of your life in retirement. Advances in medicine and technology have made it possible for people to live longer and healthier lives. People can expect to be retired longer, and that means we need to be more aware of the dangers that can take a bite out of our hard-earned savings. One of those is the high cost of assisted living or nursing care, something we'll discuss in more detail in Chapter 10. No one wants to think about living out one's years in a nursing home, but it can happen. I am sure you know someone who has needed long-term care; we all do. I speak from personal experience: my mother-in-law, at the young age of 73, has been in the nursing home for almost three years with severe Alzheimer's. These things happen, and we need to consider the possibilities in order to be prepared if they do occur. How would the cost of nursing home care affect your retirement savings? What choices do you have?

I know that sounds like a bleak and dreary road. That's not the purpose of this book. I'm not trying to

Chapter 2. Your Retirement Dream

scare you, or drive you to make a bad decision based on emotion. Quite the opposite! I want you to make good decisions based on facts. Be aware of negative possibilities, but don't let them control you. Don't let the emotion of anticipating the worst cause you to make decisions that will keep you from fulfilling your retirement dream. Don't be like Walter and Ilse, whose fear is so great that they're afraid to even enjoy their retirement at all. And don't be like Gary and Julie, whose unrealistic expectations have put them at real risk of running out of money.

Enjoy your life. Look at those dreams you have, use them as a goal, and set up a plan that will realistically allow you to accomplish those dreams without having to worry about outliving your money.

That's *my* goal for this book: to help you make a plan that will allow you to preserve your standard of living for the rest of your life, and live out your retirement dream.

The Retirement Umbrella

Chapter 3.
How Much Can You Afford to Lose?

So where do we start to build that plan, the one that will make your retirement dream a reality? If you are expecting to rely on investments, there's something you should know: The stock market is a great deceiver. Have you ever heard of the term *drawdown*? That's the percentage of loss from top to bottom in a given year of a bad market. How long will it take you to recover from a huge drawdown? Do you need, and can you afford, to take such a risk?

I often find that people have two serious misperceptions about the market: one, the rates of return that they actually receive on their market investments; and two, the risk they're willing to accept to get those returns.

I hear it all the time. People tell me that they can accept more risk, or they are willing to take more risk, or they are comfortable with risk—to achieve higher gains. But when we take a deeper look at their portfolio, we find that they're not necessarily getting the kind of gains that they thought they were getting. And that they're not really willing to accept the kind of risk that they thought they were willing to take.

Remember that the time value of money can never be replaced. With every year that passes, you have less time to build your retirement resources.

What I always ask people is this: What is the maximum percentage that you are comfortable with losing? You know that the market goes up and down. And when it does go down, many people have the idea that it will come right back up, so they think it's no big deal. But when you're getting closer to retirement, it becomes a bigger deal. You have to ask yourself, how much am I willing to lose to try to get a bigger gain? When I ask that of my clients, I often get an answer that is very different from their real comfort zone.

Let me tell you about another couple, whom we will call Tom and Susan. They are a married couple who attended one of my workshops and requested a meeting to discuss their finances: where their money was invested, what they wanted to do with it, how they wanted it to grow, the type of returns they wanted to get, and their tolerance for risk.

I started with my question. "What is the maximum percentage that you are comfortable with losing?

Chapter 3. How Much Can You Afford to Lose?

Consider what would happen if the market takes another hit and goes down again. What percentage of loss do you think you'd be comfortable with before you start getting nervous?" Susan told me, "20 percent." "Okay," I said, "20 percent, that's quite a bit of money." I had reviewed their portfolio, and 20 percent of Tom and Susan's portfolio was $160,000 dollars.

When I told them the actual dollar amount, they were shocked. Susan jumped back, and said, "Whoa, I never thought of it in the dollars and cents. That's a lot of money!" I said, "Yes, that's a lot of money, but that's 20 percent of what your portfolio is today. So if it goes down 20 percent, you're telling me you're comfortable with that. Is that true?" And she said, "Absolutely not. I'm not comfortable with that." So I asked again. "What amount of money are you comfortable with losing?" She came back with, "I'm not comfortable with losing anything."

I said, "Then you can't really be in the stock market, can you?" She said, "Okay, maybe five percent, what is that?" Well, 5 percent of their portfolio is still a lot of money, but it's not as bad as 20 percent, obviously.

The bottom line is this: When I took the percentage that Tom and Sue thought they would be comfortable with losing and put a real dollar value on it, their perspective changed completely. They realized that if they were to lose $160,000 so close to their retirement, it could take them years to recover that money. If they have to pull income from their investments prior to the market recovering, they may never recover it.

So in planning we need to look at the reality of what people in the market are possibly going to face. When the market goes down, it is going to take your future income—and potentially your standard of living—with it. Don't risk your future standard of living on an uncertainty like the stock market. There are too many good strategies out there that have been specifically designed to protect your core income, especially over the last several years with all the baby boomers who are starting to retire.

What Happens as the Baby Boomers Retire?

The United States has a huge population of baby boomers—that is, people who were born between 1946 and 1964. The Census Bureau estimates that there are about 75 million baby boomers,[2] and we're starting to see them turn 65 at the rate of 10,000 per day.[3] As they retire they're going to be pulling money from the market, from their 401(k)s, from their IRAs, and from all of the various assets that they have been accumulating over the years.

Chapter 3. How Much Can You Afford to Lose?

My fear is that 75 million people pulling money from the stock market to maintain their standard of living could have a huge negative effect, driving down the overall market. It could become a Catch-22: people pulling money out of the market to live on, and at the same time, the market going down because of people pulling money out to live on. That scenario may not bode well for people who are really looking to live comfortably in retirement.

We can't count on the market returning the kind of big gains that the '90s gave us. The '90s are long gone and I don't expect them to come back, especially as we look at how many people are going to be pulling income from the stock market over the next many, many years.

To drive the market and to maintain growth in the market, we are going to need the younger generations to invest money into the market. I don't see that happening. I don't see the next generations—the Gen Xers, born between 1965 and 1980, or the Millennials, aka Gen Yers, born between 1981 and 1997—necessarily saving a lot of money. I see them spending a lot of money. Our parents and grandparents were the generation of savers; our kids now are a generation of spenders. They are used to buying everything on credit without having to wait for what they want or to save for it. They're not saving money. In most cases, they're not even looking at long-term savings.

So if younger generations continue to keep their money out of the market, and if baby boomers continue to pull their money out, that doesn't bode well for a strong market moving forward. Quite the opposite, in fact. I expect that for years to come we will continue to see volatility in the market just as we have since the year 2000.

The moral of the story is this: Do not count on the stock market to provide you with a guaranteed income that will protect your standard of living. The market is for growth and it will let you down quite often. Remember the question I asked in a previous chapter: Is it more important for your money to grow, or for it not to shrink? Your answer will tell you how much risk you are really willing to accept in your portfolio. The market may go south when you're close to retirement, or when you're right on the verge of drawing income from your investments.

The Myth of the Magic Number

You can turn on the TV anytime and hear one expert after another on the news and the various financial channels. They constantly tout your being in the market and growing your money. They'll ask, "What's your magic number? What number do you need to achieve to reach everything you've envisioned in retirement? What is that magic number?" And the reality is I don't believe that there is a magic number. The number we're going after—the question each of us needs to answer—is this: How much core income do I need in order to maintain my standard of living for the rest of my life? If I'm married, how much do my spouse and I need to maintain our standard of living for the rest of both our lives? You don't necessarily need millions of dollars to achieve that. You just need to have a source that will provide you with a core income such that you never have to worry about outliving your income.

The TV ads and the financial pundits advise you to be in the market, but they present an unrealistic way of looking at the market.

Why take more risk than you have to? What you really need to find out is what your realistic rate is. What are your expectations? If your expectation is that you want to get a twelve percent return, well, you're going to have to take an awful lot of risk to get that twelve percent. In my role as a fiduciary, putting my client's need first, I'm going to ask you whether you need that twelve percent return to protect your standard of living. And in almost every case, the answer is no. You don't necessarily need to get a bigger return; you just have to make sure that you don't go backwards in your process of accumulating your wealth or setting up your future core income.

Don't take more risk than you need. That's a poor choice that causes unnecessary risk. Be careful when you see all the advertisements and all the different shows that are trying to tell you that you need to be in the market. They're often promoting their interests, not necessarily yours.

You may find that you are willing to accept more risk. In some cases, people really need their money to grow in order to provide them with a future income that will maintain their standard of living for the rest of their lives. If that's the case for you, then you have to be willing to accept the possibility that if you get hit with a market downturn, your retirement date may have to change. You may be looking at a date further on down the road in order to have enough assets to maintain your standard of living.

Chapter 4.
The Big Risks

When we're seeking to protect our standard of living in retirement, we need to consider a number of different risk factors that can take a big bite out of our investments and our hard-earned savings.

As we discussed in the previous chapter, one of those factors is **market risk**. I find many people have a poor understanding of what their investments have really provided them and the kind of returns that they're getting. Since the year 2000, we've seen this market go up and down, up and down, over and over. In truth, the overall growth of the stock market in this entire period of time has been diminished. It's nowhere near what people think it is. For example, in mutual funds that people have held for years, the returns are often much less than what they expected or even thought they were.

Let me give you a rough sketch. We won't talk about specific investments here, but I will give you a 30,000-foot overview. I suggest you look up your own mutual funds and get the facts. I like to use Yahoo Finance, as it provides you with good basic facts on the inner workings for your funds. Certainly there are other tools that can be used from a variety of internet sources, software providers, and investment companies, but we will keep it simple here.

Some of the most well-known, popular, and long-lived mutual funds have not provided the returns you might have expected—or been led to believe they would provide. In the 90's, most growth mutual funds did incredibly well. But over the 16-year period since the year 2000, the rate of return on some growth mutual funds is actually negative. Even the positive returns for many of the growth funds are greatly diminished—one or two percent average return during that period. You might think that a growth mutual fund, given the amount of risk it has, would offer a much bigger return. But that's not always the case.

Let me emphasize that you should look on Yahoo Finance yourself and plug in some of your own mutual funds. Look at the chart going back to the end of the 90's. There will be no hiding the facts. Some have done well. But in most cases, they experienced huge losses in 2000–2002 and 2008. Those losses caused the investor to "go backwards." Even considering the growth since 2013, those investors needed several years just to get back to the break-even line. These are very prominent funds,

Chapter 4. The Big Risks

ones you'll find in many IRA's, 401k's, brokerage accounts, etc.

A couple came to see me recently—I'll call them Owen and Barbara. They had done very well with their savings and investments, but they came to me because they were uncomfortable with the level of risk they felt the market was giving them. They wanted to make sure that they weren't going to lose a lot of money just before retirement.

So I asked them what kind of returns they had gotten. Barbara—who pretty much handled the finances—said, "Oh, we've done very well." I asked what she considered *very well*. She told me that some of her stocks had been doing about a 10 percent return or better, and I agreed that was pretty good— especially given the kind of volatility that the market has experienced. These holdings were in mutual funds. When she gave me the names of the mutual funds I pulled them right up on Yahoo Finance and said, "Well, let's take a look at how they've done since January 1 of 2000. I understand that you may or may not have owned these funds that long, but what I want to review is how they have done in both strong times and poor times. People are so quick to jump on a mutual fund based on how well it has done in the past, but aren't so quick to base their decision on how poor it may have done. Markets seem to have a life of their own, and cycles do seem to repeat."

When we looked at the real returns that she's gotten on those funds, they were, in some cases, negative. In other cases, there was a slight positive, one or two percent average return over that period of time. Barbara was in shock. She didn't even want to believe it. She thought they had been doing really well, because recently the funds had been going up. Well, they have been going up, but a lot of that rise was recovering what had previously been lost. It's a common misconception. People see their portfolio going up in value and they believe that they're actually growing their money. But in fact, they're not really growing their money: they're just recovering what they've lost. Owen and Barbara are not going to grow their money until everything gets back to its previous high point, and then it compounds above that. Then they can start saying that they've achieved some gains. So what's the real rate of return? That's the problem.

With the stock market it's critically important to look not just at the rate of return but also the **sequence of returns** in the market. The sequence of returns is the change in the rate of return that we get from year to year as the market goes up and down.

The sequence of returns is extremely important because you don't know when those negative years are going to hit, and that timing can have an enormous effect on your investment.

Chapter 4. The Big Risks

The sequence of returns chart below illustrates the impact of sequence risk on two identical portfolios over a 20-year period. Both start with the same amount of principal, experience the same rate of inflation, and draw out the same amount of income each year. Over 20 years, both have the same average rate of return, even though there are some years of double-digit losses and others of double-digit gains. But in the end Portfolio A triples in value, while Portfolio B runs out of money after only 18 years.

What's the difference? In the case of Portfolio A, the negative returns hit later, after the value has already increased substantially. With Portfolio B, the sequence is reversed. When the negative returns come early, the initial value is decreased and the later positive returns aren't enough to recover what has been lost, much less produce an overall gain.

[See Sequence of Returns chart on following pages.]

Sequence of Returns

Starting Principal: $500,000

Income: 5% of first year principal

Inflation: 3%

If you averaged 8.43% return over 20 years does the sequence of the gains and losses matter?

The only difference is that the order of returns is reversed!

Sequence risk is for real and you better be aware of it!

Age	Annual Return	Portfolio A Year-End Value	Annual Return	Portfolio B Year-End Value
66	31.69%	$ 633,450	-37.00%	$ 290,000
67	-3.11%	$ 588,000	5.49%	$ 280,171
68	30.47%	$ 740,641	15.84%	$ 298,028
69	7.62%	$ 769,760	4.91%	$ 285,343
70	10.08%	$ 819,214	10.88%	$ 288,251
71	1.32%	$ 801,047	28.68%	$ 341,941
72	37.58%	$ 1,072,231	-22.10%	$ 236,523
73	22.96%	$ 1,287,670	-11.88%	$ 177,680
74	33.36%	$ 1,685,569	-9.11%	$ 129,826
75	28.58%	$ 2,123,686	21.04%	$ 124,523
76	21.04%	$ 2,550,228	28.58%	$ 126,516
77	-9.11%	$ 2,283,299	33.36%	$ 134,117
78	-11.88%	$ 1,976,402	22.96%	$ 128,119
79	-22.10%	$ 1,502,906	37.58%	$ 138,563
80	28.68%	$ 1,896,126	1.32%	$ 119,041
81	10.88%	$ 2,063,479	10.08%	$ 92,092
82	4.91%	$ 2,124,679	7.62%	$ 58,994
83	15.84%	$ 2,419,910	30.47%	$ 35,650
84	5.49%	$ 2,510,204	-3.11%	$ -
85	-37.00%	$ 1,537,593	31.69%	$ -
8.43%				

You have to have a realistic outlook on what your funds are <u>going</u> to do and what they <u>have</u> done. Past performance isn't necessarily any guarantee of future results, but it is something we should look at, to see the negative side. When I choose investments to put together a portfolio, I go back in history. I examine not only the good years, but also the bad years. I want to look at how bad it got in 2008, and how bad it got in 2000, 2001, and 2002. Even though I didn't own the investment back then, I want to know how it performed. If we go through times like those again, how am I going to feel? Can I handle that kind of a loss? If the mutual fund that I've chosen got hit with a 45 percent loss in 2008, and that happens again, how am I going to feel? Or a better question is: How will it affect my standard of living? What will it do to my income?

That's what we need to find out. Let's not choose our investments based on past positive performance. Let's choose our investments based on how comfortable we are with the past losses that they've had. If we ask ourselves how such a loss would affect our income, that makes it a little more realistic. We are definitely going to get hit with losses. It's just a matter of how much we can handle.

We've talked a lot here about the risks of the stock market, but that's only one of several big risks that can wash out your hard-earned money. They are many other dangers that make your retirement umbrella so essential. Market risk is one of them, and now let's take a look at some others.

Chapter 4. The Big Risks

Taxes – Let's face it, taxes will inevitably affect your retirement plan in some way. When we save for retirement, we generally save in tax-deferred accounts, in hopes that when we retire, we'll be in a lower tax bracket than during our working years. We expect that once we retire and begin to pull funds out of these accounts, we won't have to pay as much taxes on them. But that's not a guarantee. It's possible that we could be in a higher tax bracket when we retire.

As of the writing of this book, we're actually at a point here in the United States where our tax brackets are not as bad as they have been in the past. There is some uncertainty, however, about where our tax brackets are going to go. You may recall that back in the late '70s, we had tax brackets that were just ridiculous (in my opinion). That could happen again. And if it does happen again, when you retire and begin to withdraw the money that you've been saving in your 401(k) and your IRA, you could be paying taxes on that money at a higher tax bracket than the one you're in now. What will you do if that happens?

One way to reduce taxes on your income is to work with a CPA who will do a "tax-forward" plan for you. Most people who work with a CPA pay them to do the taxes for the past year. Tax-forwarding is working with a CPA to determine how you can lower your taxes for the current year.

One more word on taxes: You also need to beware of phantom income tax. That's a tax you pay on capital gains and/or dividends from a mutual fund in a year when the mutual fund actually went down in value. You may have experienced that in your non-qualified or non-IRA accounts.

Inflation – We have to keep up with inflation. Right now, our cost of living adjustments for inflation are low, and I think they are deceptive. When I go to the supermarket today, it costs me more to buy the goods and foods that I bought in the past. It costs me a lot more today than it did 5 or 10 years ago.

Let's think about it. I was born in 1960. The average income in 1960 was just under $5,200 a year. $5,200 dollars a year! It's almost unfathomable that anybody could ever possibly live on that for an entire year. Back then, everything was a lot cheaper. A new home only cost $12,600; a brand new car was $2,600.

Everything cost a lot less money, but incomes were substantially lower.

Let's fast-forward 20 years. Now we're in 1980. In 1980, the average income went all the way up to $19,173. That's a pretty substantial boost in income over that 20-year period. But what happened to the home cost? The same new home that cost a little over $12,000 dollars in 1960 cost $68,700 in 1980. A new car went from $2,600 to $7,200. That's a pretty substantial difference over those 20 years; while our incomes quadrupled, our expenses jumped as well.

How have things changed since then? Let's see. When was the last time you saw a five-and-dime store? Today we have dollar stores, or even five-dollar stores. You sure cannot find a new car for $7,200. You'd be lucky to find a really good used car for that kind of money.

Will your money keep up with inflation? When you start drawing income from your pension, is your pension going to keep pace with inflation? Keep in mind that a $50,000 income today will probably need to be about $65-70,000 in 15 years just to have the same buying power.

Inflation is one of those factors that will always be with us. We also have to take into account the effect of hidden inflation—where the cost of our items stays the same, but the items themselves get smaller. Just an example: When's the last time you saw a half gallon of ice cream? You can't even buy one anymore.

Combine inflation with taxes, and those two things can take a big bite out of your retirement income.

Health Care – I can't emphasize enough how devastating health care risk can be. As I just mentioned, people are living longer and longer. In many cases, this is because of advances in medicine.

This is great in helping extend our lives, but unfortunately it can be *very* expensive. I can speak firsthand, as my family has unfortunately had some pretty significant health care issues. I know how extremely expensive it can be when you have to have surgeries, or when you have to make other hospital visits. We've also had the unfortunate experience of having to place my mother-in-law into a nursing home. Long-term care is extremely expensive.

Health care is an x-factor. We can't know what to expect in terms of our health care needs and costs, or how it will affect our income, or how much of our income might have to be directed to health care expenses. We don't know what our insurance costs will be. We do see the cost of care going up; we see the cost of drugs going up. That's not going to slow down, and it can become a bigger and bigger threat to your income and therefore to your standard of living.

But wait! There are still additional factors we need to consider.

Interest – As of the writing of this book, interest rates are really low, which is good for people who want to borrow money. It's not so good for people who want good, sound, safe investments in the banks, because they can't give good returns. Dave Scranton, the author of a book called *Stop the Financial Insanity*, describes the interest rate environment today as "working capital not working."[4] It's humorous, yet true. Low interest rates are great for people who are borrowing money, but horrible for people who want to put their money into CDs and safe-haven types of bank investments. They're not getting anything back from them, and that's the problem with interest rates being so low. This is your working capital—your cash accounts, the money that you need to pay for everyday expenses or for unforeseen expenses. You need a roof on the house; you need to put new windows in; you need to do something with your driveway; you have a family crisis. You have to have money in reserve to be able to pay for any of these things, but it's sitting in the bank earning—what? Right now, nothing.

There are also rumors that interest rates may even go negative. What in the world is a negative interest rate? A negative interest rate means we pay the bank for holding our money. How would you like that? At that point, I think we'd find a lot of people buying waterproof safes and burying their money in the backyard. That would be better than keeping it in the bank and paying a fee for it. Where will interest rates take us next? Will they go up? If they go up, that's great for people who are saving money.

My parents weren't able to save a lot, because my dad didn't make a whole lot, but they did inherit a little bit of money from my grandparents. When they did that, they invested it into a CD. My dad was never a risk-taker. He never wanted to put any money in the stock market, and never did. He never owned any stock, any bonds, or any mutual funds. When he inherited a little bit of money, he put it into a CD. The CDs were paying 16 and 17 percent returns. Your money grows pretty fast when you've got a safe haven like that paying such big interest rates. It was great for my parents, but on the other side of that, those high rates weren't so good for people who were buying houses back then. You need to take interest rates into account—how are they likely to affect you going forward into retirement?

Probate – What will happen to your assets when you die? If you want to pass them on to your heirs, you will need to take probate into account. If your estate is not set up properly, there are many things that can create expenses and delays in the probate process, not to mention the additional stress on your heirs in the wake of your passing. When we get into a little more advanced planning, and start looking at how to pass on assets in the most efficient way, we want to try to avoid probate. There are some really good strategies for doing that. I won't go into detail in this chapter, but it is an area to consider in protecting your assets.

Procrastination – We talked about procrastination in the previous chapter, but it's worth noting again

Chapter 4. The Big Risks

here, because it really is one of the biggest risks to your retirement standard of living. Most people are aware of the various risks out there. They may even be worried about them. But they just don't want to deal with them. It's easier to pretend that if they ignore them long enough, the risks will just go away. But the fact is, they don't go away. The risks actually get worse if you don't deal with them. If you're not prepared, some of these things can wipe out your retirement income before you are ready to draw from it. That's why you need to make a retirement plan and stick with it.

I like to use the analogy of a Retirement Umbrella. Our umbrella protects us—and our belongings—from sudden rains, or unforeseen storms, or any of the things that can rain down on our hard-earned money. Truth is, I'm not a big umbrella guy in my day-to-day life. I don't normally carry one—but I can tell you that I've been caught in the rain on many occasions. On the other hand, my wife is always prepared. She usually has an umbrella available. Hence, she's the one who doesn't get wet when the rain starts pouring down—I do. I may be wearing a pretty nice shirt, so when it starts to sprinkle, I'm all spotted with rain. If I had kept an umbrella nearby like my wife did, I would have stayed dry.

That's what your retirement umbrella will do. It will protect you—and your standard of living—from those inevitable financial rains. Taxes, inflation and market risk are always going to be present. You know at least one of those three factors will likely throw a monkey wrench in your finances. Now imagine what would happen to your standard of living if several of them occurred at once. Example: The stock market takes a 30% hit, when inflation is up to 7%, right after a tax increase; now add a health care or family crisis. We cannot possibly prevent these events from occurring; however, we certainly can have a plan in the event that they do happen.

You can see the signs of stormy weather. You can see the rainclouds on the horizon. You can see the sky getting darker, and you know that means rain is likely. Do you have an umbrella to safeguard you from the rainstorm? Your retirement umbrella will do just that: It will protect you against unanticipated healthcare expenses, or an unfortunately-timed drop in the stock market, or inflation going out of control, or rising taxes. Be prepared. Have that umbrella handy.

One more big reason to have that umbrella handy is longevity. Remember that the number one fear is running out of money. Will your money last as long as you do? Do you have a plan that will carry you through the end of your life—and in the case of a married couple, the rest of *both* your lives?

Longevity – We already talked about the fastest growing segment of our population, the Baby

Chapter 4. The Big Risks

Boomers. How many people do you know who are age 85 and up? I have numerous clients who fall into that category, and the number is growing rapidly. My own mother has reached 92 and counting, and still lives a pretty active life. I had a client who is 85 and up until recently was taking care of her mother, who reached 102 before she passed away. How would you like to be a caregiver at age 85? It could happen. We live in what some call the sandwich generation. That is, we have kids (who are younger and still need help), but in addition we have parents (who are aging and need assistance). Many of the diseases that would take lives in the past are now being treated and in many cases cured. That is a blessing; but on the other hand, we may need assistance in our later years, when in the past we would have already passed away.

The Retirement Umbrella

Chapter 5.
The Traditional Path

Chances are that up to now, you've been following what I call a traditional path in your retirement savings. But that traditional path may not be the most effective in meeting your needs and protecting your standard of living. The traditional path is often driven by our emotions. In this chapter, I want to challenge some of the thinking that puts so many people on that path.

Another couple, whom we will call Bill and Eileen, came into my office recently. They wanted me to review their 401(k) plan with them. Bill pulled out the several pages of 401(k) choices that he had and we looked at his overall portfolio. As I was looking it over, I recognized many of the mutual funds in the portfolio. I asked him, "How did you choose these investments?" I knew what the answer would be before he even gave it to me. Sure enough, it was exactly what I thought he'd say: "I chose them based on the best performing mutual funds over the last three to five years." Bill and Eileen were definitely on a traditional path in their 401(k).

Bill had chosen the best performing mutual funds based on past performance. That's very, very common. It's also a big mistake, partly because it's based on emotions. Here's why: Past performance is no guarantee of future results. You'll see that disclaimer in all of the literature and all of the TV advertisements, and it's ABSOLUTLY true. It's important to take that seriously because mutual funds almost never repeat their past performance. Take a look at some of the financial magazines, websites, and other sources that publish reports of the best performing mutual funds over the last 5 years, 10 years, or 20 years. You'll see one list of mutual funds, then a completely different list five years later. They almost never repeat.

When you look at the past performance of the investment choices inside many 401(k)s, you'll find that they are fairly similar to each other. The reason is that mutual fund managers buy and sell stock based on analytical data. They read statistics about stocks, about price-earnings ratios, about various companies and their management. They use all of this data to determine whether or not they're going to buy or sell a particular stock.

Keep in mind that all of these fund managers are reading very similar data. So it stands to reason that they're buying and selling a lot of the same stocks at the same times. This is very common—we call it overlap, when many fund managers own a lot of the same stocks. As a participant in the fund, you paid to buy the stock (called a transitional cost), you may have paid to sell the same stock in a different mutual fund and you didn't even know you owned it. That happens all the time inside of your mutual funds.

Here's a better scenario for you, if you're looking to build up a really good portfolio. Remember that when you're in the buying mode, you're accumulating assets and shares. You're not looking to sell or to draw income from your portfolio. So if you're looking to accumulate assets, do you want to buy shares at a discount or do you want to pay a premium for them? The answer is obvious: You want to buy them at a discount. Think of it like the old blue light special at Kmart: two pairs of tennis shoes for the price of one. It works the same way when you're buying stocks.

When you look at the mutual funds and stocks inside of your portfolio and you're looking to just accumulate, then shouldn't you be looking for the best deals? That means looking at the stocks that are not doing as well. Those are the ones that you probably should be buying. Don't misunderstand me: I'm not saying dump all your good holdings and buy all the junk. You need to look at your overall portfolio and consider putting a portion of your holdings in safer investments and then buy into the ones that aren't doing as well. Now before you jump up and make a complete overhaul of your 401k you need to look at the options that are available determine how similar they may be. But in my opinion if you are in the accumulation phase and you're going to buy shares in the stock market, buy the ones that are on sale. Traditional thinking says focus on the stocks that are doing well. I'm saying, don't just buy the ones that have done incredibly well because they probably only have one direction to go. If you're looking to grow the value of your portfolio, take a good look at the holdings in it and reconsider your buying strategy. Now understand that using this strategy really requires that you first protect a large portion of your principal. Then buy into the riskier funds with your new deposits. That's one step off of the traditional path.

Getting Off the Beaten Path

Let's look a little more closely at that traditional path. What does it really mean? This is the basic thinking. During our working years, the traditional path is to save money out of your paycheck, reduce your taxable income by putting money into your 401(k) plan, and pay taxes on that money later, when you have retired and expect to be in a lower tax bracket. That all sounds well and good, doesn't it? The traditional plan is to always be saving into your retirement account or qualified plan and then stay

Chapter 5. The Traditional Path

the course—ride out the ups and downs of the market—expecting that the market will always recover. Traditional thinking says that you haven't really lost anything until you have sold. And that's true, but no one talks about the flip side, which is that you haven't gained anything until you have sold either.

Suppose you receive a monthly statement that shows you have been hit with a 20 percent loss due to a stock market "correction." (I hate that industry term. Was it "incorrect" when it was going up?) You may tell yourself—or your advisor may tell you—that it's only a paper loss. Well, when the market goes up 20 percent, remember it's only a paper gain. **The only way that you can compound a gain and lock in that gain, is to sell.** That's a big problem for many people. They don't know when to sell. Inside their 401(k) plans, people don't often make adjustments. When the market is going up, they just watch it rise and they feel really good when they see their 401(k) getting larger and larger. Then all of sudden they get hit with a 30 or 40 percent loss. Why didn't they lock in some of those gains when they saw them? Why didn't they protect that principal? They were victims of traditional thinking—which you'll hear on the news and in many financial publications—that says, "Stay the course." And because they stayed the course, they did not take those paper gains and turn them into actual gains.

The Retirement Umbrella

The traditional path tells you to stay the course. I am telling you this: Consider protecting some of your gains. Or to put it another way, don't be afraid to take your winnings off the table. (The better path is to never lose in the first place).

Let me tell you another story that will show you just what I mean.

Some years ago, I was in Las Vegas for a series of meetings. In between our meetings, a friend of mine and I went for a walk around the casino floor of the Bellagio. I am always amazed watching the people who gamble. What really amazes me is that every time I talk to someone who has just come back from Vegas, and I ask them how they did, they usually tell me they broke even. I guess nobody has ever lost a dime in Las Vegas. How is that?

Isn't that remarkable? You look at all that the casinos have built: the beautiful fountains, the spectacular architecture, all the lights, and everything else. But nobody ever loses any money there. Or so they'll tell you.

As I was watching people at various gaming tables, I became intrigued by a gentleman who was playing the craps table. I don't know much about craps and my friend was trying to explain it to me. I had no idea that there were so many possible bets and combinations of bets to be made. In the midst of my friend's explanation, which was mostly going over my head, I kept watching this one gentleman as he was playing the game. He had a large pile of chips in front of him and a larger pile of chips off to the side.

I saw that he had bets all over the table. He was winning some and losing some. I noticed that every time he won he would take the winnings and he would put them off to the side in that growing pile. The chips in front of him were the only chips that he used to play. He never touched the chips off to the side, just kept adding to them when he won. What he was doing, obviously, was hedging his bets. He had bets all over the table and when he did well with a bet and he won, he took those winnings off the table and parked them. Then he might reposition into a different bet with the chips he had in front of him but he never touched the chips off to the side.

It dawned on me that his strategy was exactly what we should be doing with our investments. We should be locking in our gains and protecting them from future losses (building that pile up), while we continue to accumulate chips without putting our gains at risk. So again, the only money we would put at risk is the money that we use to buy in. This strategy is similar to what I suggested at the beginning of this chapter. If you have a 401(k), IRA or other long-term investments in the market, consider this strategy to reduce your market exposure. Always review the pros and cons with your advisor and remember, you might have had an even greater gain if you had stayed the course with your current investments, but remember our basic question: Is it more important for your money to grow, or for it not to shrink? Do you want to get good returns but also keep them, or do you want to just roll the dice and see how big of a return you can get? One is a logical choice; the other is emotional. If it's the latter, you have to be willing to accept the possibility that your portfolio could drop 40 percent the year before your retirement. Would you be okay with that? I certainly wouldn't, and neither would most of my clients. So what we want to do is make sure that you're protecting some of those gains. Put that pile off to the side. Don't take the traditional path and just stay the course. We know that the market always goes up and down, so let's use that to our advantage. When it goes up, don't be afraid to sell shares. Protect your gains. Put them off to the side. When the market goes down, buy more shares. Protecting your gains will help you protect your standard of living for the long term.

The Managing Risk Graphic below is one I use with my clients to illustrate what I mean about protecting your income and your gains. I call it the three-bucket model for investing.

Chapter 5. The Traditional Path

The green bucket is safe and simple. It won't be affected by a negative stock market but its rate of return is limited. This bucket contains the money to be used for your main source of guaranteed income. The percentage of your investment money you put there should be based on your comfort zone. The yellow bucket is low risk—not no risk, but low risk. You can use this bucket to supplement your income but you need to be careful as it does not carry guarantees and will go up and down. The red bucket is the highest risk bucket and also the highest return potential. I do not recommend that you draw income from this bucket unless the market is high and you want to preserve your gains. This is where you put the money that you can afford to risk. Again, it's important to be careful here. You can put as much as

MANAGING RISK

CAS CREATIVE ASSET SOLUTIONS
PLANS THAT WORK. PEOPLE WHO CARE.

HOW MUCH RISK DO YOU WANT?

Emergency Funds	Safe & Secure Assets	Low Risk Investment	Moderate Risk Investment
6-9 MONTHS OF EXPENSES	_____ %	_____ %	_____ %
Checking Accts Savings Accts CDs Money Market	Goal 4-5% per year Over 5-10 years	Goal 6-8% per year Over 5-10 years	Goal 9-10% per year Over 5-10 years
100% Liquid Very Low Returns 0-2% per year			

WHAT IS THE MAXIMUM LOSS YOU WOULD ACCEPT BEFORE YOU WOULD BEGIN TO FEEL VERY UNCOMFORTABLE? _____% WHAT IS THAT DOLLAR AMOUNT? _____

Advisory Services offered through Bridgeriver Advisors, LLC, Member FINRA/SIPC, and a Registered Investment Advisor.

you want in this bucket as long as you have money in the other two buckets that will protect your income and standard of living. When you have a big gain in the red bucket, you can protect your gain by moving it out of the red bucket and into one of the other two.

I can give you an example from my own personal experience. I have an account that I call my play account. I don't look at it very often, but I do buy and sell inside of it once in a while. If it goes up, that's great. If it goes down, it's not going to affect my standard of living. Well, I bought a stock based on some research that I had found. It was a stock that was predicted to go way up, and after I bought it, it did just that. It went way up. I took a look at the account and I noticed that this stock had gone up almost two hundred percent in about six months. My first thought, naturally, was, "wow, that thing is doing incredibly well. I wonder how much higher it will go." Then it dawned on me: that was greed talking (a big emotion). I saw a big gain and wanted a bigger gain. When I came to my senses, and used some logic, I realized that I needed to protect some of that two hundred percent. The only way to protect it was to sell off some of that stock because it probably couldn't really go much higher. It did go slightly higher, and then it started to come down, but I did sell it and I sold it at a very big gain.

Chapter 5. The Traditional Path

I protected my gains and I put them into something that would be less risky if the market goes down. I recognized the greed talking—it's often greed that prevents us from making good, logical decisions.

We talked earlier in the book about the danger of making decisions based on emotion. Greed is another one of those emotions that can lead to bad decisions. Greed has no logic, and when we get greedy, we take unnecessary risks that can impact our retirement and our future standard of living.

When is a Dollar not a Dollar?

There's another point that we need to consider when we're talking about the traditional path of saving money into our 401(k)s or other retirement vehicles. While we're working, we reduce our income and our taxes by putting money into these accounts, but at some point we're going to be pulling money out of them. What often gets overlooked is the fact that when you pull a dollar out of your 401(k) plan it's not a dollar. It's a dollar minus taxes. That means your net return—what goes in your pocket—is going to be less than a dollar. The exact return will depend on what your tax bracket is when you pull that dollar out.

Let's look at another client, whom we will call Rita. Rita's story is a great example of not understanding the tax ramifications of an IRA. When Rita came to me she had recently been widowed. Her husband had handled all the finances and after he passed away, it all fell into her lap. She was unfamiliar with the different types of investments; she didn't know what an IRA was; she didn't understand taxes. He had handled all of that. After he passed away, Rita decided that she was going to buy a new car. She had wanted one for a while and decided it was time to get the car she had always wanted. She called me up and said, "I need $40,000 to buy this new car and I'd like to take money out of my husband's IRA to do that."

I looked at the amount that she had in the IRA. I said, "Well, you have enough money to pull $40,000 out but do you understand that when you pull $40,000 out, you're not going to get $40,000? You have to pay taxes on it." I had to explain to her that the taxes on that $40,000 would reduce her net to $25,000-30,000, and that she would have to pull close to $60,000 to get $40,000 cash for the car. I said, "Is it worth $60,000 to own that car?" I pointed out that it would reduce her portfolio by a substantial margin, and suggested some other options: buying a less expensive car, or taking out a zero interest car loan and taking income from the IRA to pay the loan instead of taking it all out in one lump sum and paying all those taxes in one year.

Chapter 5. The Traditional Path

For Rita, that was a real revelation. Like many people, she had never thought about the fact that she would have to pay taxes on any money she pulled out of an IRA. **Always remember this: A dollar is not a dollar when you're taking it out of a retirement vehicle.** A part of it will be going to Uncle Sam. When you look at the money that you have in your retirement vehicles—your 401(k), IRA, 403(b), 457 or any of those types of retirement plans—remember that each time you draw money out, you will be paying some portion, depending on your tax bracket, back to the government. These vehicles are not tax-free; they're tax-deferred. The system gives you a tax break while you are working by deferring taxes in hopes that once you retire you'll be in a lower tax bracket. Depending on what the government does with tax rates, that may or may not be the case.

Let's understand something very clearly here. The government can change tax rates at any time. If that happens, your standard of living is going to be affected. It could cost you more to pull money out of these savings and investments that you've been accumulating all of these years. How will taxes affect your standard of living? Where are you going to get the additional money that you need? That's where your retirement umbrella comes in: to protect your standard of living. Retirement income planning is a lot more complex than it ever was a few years ago, not only because of taxes, but also because of all the other big risks we discussed in Chapter 4.

In reality, it's completely different from what the traditional path would have us do. When you start setting up your income, you have to take into consideration how taxes are going to reduce your income from your retirement savings. You have to be able to keep up with inflation, both expressed inflation and hidden inflation. In the future, it's going to cost you more to buy the goods and services that you want. You have to be able to keep up with additional healthcare costs. You have to consider probable tax increases. You're going to be putting less money in your pocket. Being prepared—by having a good umbrella over your entire plan— becomes critical if you want to make sure that your standard of living is going to be protected for the rest of your life.

Chapter 6.
Common Retirement Vehicles

As we work toward setting up that retirement umbrella, I want to take a quick look at the various vehicles that we use to save for retirement.

One of the most common ways to save is through an employer. As part of their employee benefits package, many employers offer some kind of retirement plan. Depending upon the employer, the type of plan will vary. It might be a 401(k), a 403(b), a 457, or some other plan. These are all what we call **corporate tax-deferred accounts**. They reduce your taxable income by the amount of money that you put into them. That amount is typically deducted from your paycheck. You can choose whether or not to participate in the employer's plan and how much of your salary to put into it. You can choose where to invest the funds, but your choices are limited to what the employer offers in the plan. When you leave that employer, or retire, it's usually a good idea to rollover the money from your 401(k) or 403(b) into a personal individual retirement account, where you can invest it into anything that you want and choose strategies that better meet your needs. That also allows you to get away from the hidden fees commonly attached to these plans.

Should you participate in your employer's plan? One good reason to participate is that many companies offer an employer match, contributing some percentage of what you put into the plan, and if they do, you should always take advantage of that. It's free money—it would be foolish not to take advantage of it. Always put money into your plan up to the amount of the employer match. If the employer match is three percent of your annual salary, then put in three percent. If there is no employer match, your employer plan may still be a good option but there are other options to consider.

If you are self-employed, or not participating in an employer's plan, you may choose to set up an **IRA (Individual Retirement Account)**. Let me add that there are other tax deferred accounts that may allow people who are self-employed to add more money into them, but for sake of space in this book I won't go into a lengthy explanation. My objective is to give a basic understanding of what an IRA is, not to give a recommendation. I think that a better understanding of any IRA is that it's an <u>individual</u> <u>retirement</u> <u>arrangement</u>. It's an arrangement you make with the

Chapter 6. Common Retirement Vehicles

federal government that says as long as you keep your money underneath this IRA umbrella you will protect it against the taxes raining down on it. You defer the taxes until later.

You might also have a **Roth IRA**. That is a tax deferred account, but unlike a traditional IRA, a Roth IRA does not reduce your taxable income when you put money into it. So when you eventually draw money out, you do so tax-free. Unlike a traditional IRA, which requires a minimum distribution at age 70 and a half, the Roth IRA has no required distribution. There are some limitations on what can be put into any of these accounts and talking to a professional is advisable before you open one up.

For some reason, people often think of IRAs as different from their investments. The other day I sat down with a new client, and asked if he had money in the stock market. He said, "No, all I have is IRAs." So I asked him where his IRA was invested, and he said, "Well, in my various different brokerage accounts, mutual funds, and things like that." I had to point out to him that the money in those accounts was money in the stock market. I often find that people mistakenly think that an IRA is an actual specific investment, when in fact it is simply a shelter from taxes like your 401(k)s, 403(b)s, 457s, etc. You can put your IRA over anything you want: stocks, bonds, mutual funds, annuities, real estate, even precious metals and gold.

Now, those last few items are things that get a lot more complex, and I'm not recommending them, just pointing out that you can literally put your IRA—your individual retirement account/arrangement—over a variety of different investments.

Think of your IRA as an umbrella. It's a shelter for your savings, protecting them from tax rains. YOU choose the investments.

The IRA is one of our sources of retirement income. Remember that in retirement we have four possible income sources: Social Security, a pension, income from full- or part-time work, and savings and investments. You need to look at all of those when you're planning how to protect your standard of living. Let's look at how that played out for one client.

A Cautionary Tale

I met some years ago with a retired gentleman, whom we will call Dave. Dave had spent his entire career as a Kmart employee. When he retired, he received a pension from Kmart. He was also drawing Social Security, so Dave had income from two of our four sources. In addition, he had a 401(k) plan, and a huge portion of that was in Kmart stock. When I met with him, I suggested that he consider selling some of it because the vast majority of all his money—$300,000—was invested in Kmart stock.

Dave told me that he had a low risk tolerance, so I asked him why he kept all of his money wrapped up in just one company's stock. His response was, "Well, Kmart's been really good to me. They provide me with my pension. They provided me with a job for over 37 years, and I want to be loyal to them." I tried to tell him while loyalty was great, that was a lot of risk to have in one company, no matter what the company.

Dave didn't take my advice. He did nothing with that money; he held onto it and didn't sell any of that stock. And unfortunately, his loyalty to the company hurt him in the end. Kmart stock went to nothing. It went to zero, and he lost every dime of that money. I hate to even tell this story because it's so sad, thinking of Dave, in his mid-80s, losing almost everything that he had saved his entire life to get. The one saving grace was the fact that between his pension and Social Security he had enough core income to sustain his standard of living for him and his wife for the rest of their lives. There's nothing extra, though. There's no money to pass on to his kids, which he would really have loved to have done. That might have been possible if he had chosen differently, but he made an emotional decision out of company loyalty. (Remember what we said about making emotional decisions?)

The moral of the story is what we said earlier: As long as enough of your income is protected to maintain your standard of living, you can take more risk in the market. But don't be foolish with the risks that you do take.

Planning Your Retirement Income

There are pros and cons to any retirement savings vehicle. And any of them can factor into your retirement planning. What I do with my clients is to help them plan for their retirement income. We look at the income they'll need to sustain their standard of living, and at the four possible income sources— Social Security, a pension, work income, and savings/investments (their IRA)—from which they can draw that income in the most tax-efficient way. That's where it can get tricky.

Understand this: Whether you put your money into a stock, a bond or a mutual fund, you will be paying taxes on that money when you pull it out. That will be based on the tax rate, and your tax bracket at the time that you pull it out. The higher the tax bracket you're in, the more taxes will be withheld, and the less money you'll put in your pocket. The less money that you put in your pocket is potentially less money that you have to protect your standard of living.

When we start looking at how much income that you're going to need, you can't forget about taxes. A client may tell me she needs $5,000 a month to sustain her standard of living. So where will we get that $5,000 a month? Well, $2,000 of it will come from Social Security. That means we need to find another $3,000. She doesn't have a pension, and she is not working. That leaves the fourth income source, savings and investments. Okay, where are her savings and investments positioned? Are they all in IRAs? If they're all in IRAs and we need to get $3,000, how much does she have to pull out of her IRA to get that $3,000? Remember, a dollar is not a dollar when you're drawing it out of your IRA.

That's just one example. You always need to look at all the different places where you can pull income. You need to make decisions using strategies specifically designed for income generation and not draw income from investments that will go up and down. You need to keep all of the big risks in mind, like inflation, unforeseen healthcare costs, family crises, interest rates, and of course longevity. The question becomes: How will you pull your core income in the most tax efficient way and provide for your standard of living for the rest of your life?

That's why it's so important to clearly understand the savings vehicles we've been using all these years and how your IRA will affect your standard of living.

Chapter 7.
Protect Your Core Income

So far, we've talked about the fears that we face in retirement planning, the big risks to our retirement income, and some of the most common ways to save for retirement—all important things to consider as we put a retirement umbrella in place. Now I want to talk about some other strategies that can become a significant piece of your retirement umbrella. That umbrella is what will protect your standard of living and make it so that you can *greatly* reduce your fears about running out of money. Wouldn't that be fantastic? I want to help you make that happen.

When we talk about protecting your core income, we must look at strategies that can protect your standard of living for rest of your life. In a husband and wife scenario we need to look at protecting your core income for the rest of *both* your lives. That means no matter what happens to the stock market, no matter what happens to the bond markets, no matter what happens, period—changing interest rates, shifting economies, or unforeseen world events, your standard of living is *protected*. I like to call it the S.W.A.N Method, because it will allow you to <u>S</u>leep

<u>W</u>ell <u>A</u>t <u>N</u>ight. Using this method, we set up a strategy that means your standard of living is protected no matter what storms come your way. I can tell you there is a great peace in being able to say, "Hey, we're okay. The stock market crashed 30 percent but it isn't going to change my standard of living."

One of the most effective ways to guarantee that your standard of living—your retirement income—will be protected, no matter what, is using annuities. *Ugh*, I know you're not ready for this. The hair on the back of your neck stands up as soon as I say the word "annuities," right?

It's okay; don't panic.

I know very well that annuities are often misrepresented and misunderstood. There are a lot of myths and misinformation associated with them. What we are going to do is to cut through all of that and get to the facts.

Annuities have been around for a long, long time. I'm sure you'll be surprised to learn that they go all the way back to ancient Rome. The word itself comes from the Latin term *annua*, meaning annual stipend. It was a contract that made annual payments. Roman citizens would make a payment into the annua and then receive a fixed annual payment for the rest of their lives. Roman soldiers were paid annuities for their military service; if they died in service, the payment went to their family. It was the emperors' way of saying, "You fight for us. We'll guarantee that your income will be protected for the rest of your family's life."

Annuities have continued to evolve over the centuries. Forms of annuities have been used by rulers and governments to finance armies, building projects, administration, and many other things.

In the Modern Era, the Union government used annuities as a compensation for soldiers who fought in the Civil War. Annuities became more popular in this country beginning in the early 20th century. Many people of great stature and wealth began to put money into annuities so that they would be guaranteed an income for the rest of their life. Babe Ruth was one of the most prominent. When the stock market crashed in 1929, he was not affected because he had invested a lot of his money into annuities to protect his income.[5]

There have been entire books written, and there will continue to be entire books written, on all different kinds of annuities. For our discussion in this chapter, we're going to focus on the most common aspects of annuities. We're going to talk about the different types of annuities, and I'm really going to focus on the safe and guaranteed aspects of what we call "fixed" or "guaranteed" annuities.

Most people don't fully understand what an annuity is. So let's start at the very beginning. What is an annuity? Basically, **an annuity is a contractual agreement with an insurance company**. The terms will vary with the type of annuity, but the essential agreement is that, if you agree to give your money to them for a set period of time, your money will grow based on the underlying investment. Originally annuities were designed to provide a guaranteed income just like a pension (immediate or pension annuity). But today annuities are used primarily as an investment or savings vehicle. Some carry market risk (variable annuities), some have fixed or guaranteed returns (fixed interest annuities), and some give you a portion of an indexed gain but zero if that index goes down in value (fixed indexed annuities). All will provide an income stream if chosen but they need to be looked at carefully in order to determine which ones might fit your needs the best.

Variable Annuities

Variable annuities have only been around since 1952. About the early '80s they became more popular. These types of annuities carry more risk, as they are invested heavily into mutual fund-like accounts. These accounts are officially called "Separate Accounts," which are technically <u>not</u>

mutual funds, even though they are just <u>like</u> mutual funds. Clear as mud, right? What this means is that your money will go up, or it will go down, based on what those investments do. If the market does well, your investment will do well. If the market goes down, your investment will go down.

Most variable annuities carry a guarantee for the death benefit: If you die and the market has gone down in the period of time you've held that contract, the death benefit will be at least what you put into it—sometimes more, depending on the structure of the death benefit. Keep in mind that you do pay a fee to get that death benefit. It's called a "mortality and expense fee," and it varies greatly from company to company. Some are quite high, and other companies may not charge that much at all. Some companies may not even offer the benefit at all, but if they do, there will be a fee associated with it.

There are also additional riders that can be attached to a variable annuity to protect the future income in the event of a stock market decline. The problem with these riders, of course, is that there are more fees associated with them but an even bigger concern should be that they are greatly misunderstood by both the consumer and in many cases even the advisor. Those fees will guarantee a certain growth rate on your account for income purposes. The guarantee does not allow you to just take that money and walk away. In almost every case you have to turn it into an income stream to get the guarantee. Most people don't realize that.

I'm not going to go into great detail about the different payouts or the different types of guarantees that variable annuities offer. The bottom line is this: **A variable annuity is a risk-type investment that offers some additional guarantees for a price**. You have to be aware of what those fees are, because they come out of your pocket. In many cases you may not even see them. They're just part of the contract. These fees can be as high as four and a half to five percent, depending on the various riders in the contract, and they vary greatly from contract to contract. You need to look at these riders with great caution. What do they offer? Does that apply to your situation? Is it worth the extra money? It may or may not be. Refer to the prospectus for all the fees associated with any variable annuity. To help better understand what these fees are I have put together a list of questions, in chapter 13, that I have used when calling insurance companies to find out specifically what the fees are.

One more word of caution: These riders don't always provide the type of benefit you think they may be providing. I highly recommend that you do an independent review of any variable annuity that you have. That means sitting down with an advisor, who will call the insurance company directly with you, and ask them some specific questions about your account. (In chapter 13 I have included a list of questions that you should know). That will help you to see if, in fact, what you have and what you're paying for is what you really want, and more importantly, what you really need.

The best advice I can give on variable annuities is be careful. In my experience, you can usually get a better income payout from another type of annuity. It's always best to compare.

Fixed or Guaranteed Annuities

This brings us to another type of annuity, which we call "fixed" or "guaranteed." These come in a couple of different flavors. One is an **immediate, or payout, or pension annuity**. This is really what most pensions are. Almost every pension is some form of annuity. Even Social Security is, in some ways, an annuity. It's an annuitized payout. You put money into the system for years while you're working and when you retire, you draw on it based on your life expectancy. You get an income stream from it for the rest of your life. Although it's not with an insurance company, it is an annuitized payout.

There are personal pension annuities. You put money into them and in return they will pay you a specific amount of money for a specific period of time. That may be a 5-year, 10-year, or 20-year period or a lifetime period. There may be several other options available for you to choose from as well. The payment is sent to you, and it will come to you no matter what. You do need to be careful in relationship to the payout terms. Once you turn them on they are usually irreversible.

I don't normally recommend immediate or pension annuities, unless they are going to be used for a specific amount of money that the client needs for a specific period of time. In that case, they may be worth considering. I just don't like the irreversibility of most of them. However, because of their tax advantages when using non-IRA accounts, they can provide a nice source of guaranteed income to supplement your other sources of retirement income. In addition, some of these annuities even offer an inflation benefit that increases your income based on the inflation factor.

That brings me to the most common type of annuity, one that has been around for many years. That is the **fixed or guaranteed annuity**. In return for a fixed interest rate of return, you leave your money with the insurance company for a set period of time determined at the beginning of the contract. It could be anything from two years to 20 years or more. You are allowed to pull money out of the annuity, but on

Chapter 7. Protect Your Core Income

a limited basis, typically 10 percent per year. Should you need the funds for a terminal illness, hospital stay, or a death, most companies offer additional withdrawal, but otherwise you are limited on the accessibility of your money. If you pass the annuity on to your beneficiary, in most cases it goes directly to your beneficiaries without any charges or fees.

The downside of a fixed annuity is that your rate of return is limited. You're not going to receive a big return. It's going to be whatever the interest rates bear in the market, and currently, interest rates are very low. Fixed annuities don't pay much, though they typically pay better than CDs. They will never build your wealth. They're safe and very simple. They are good for people who are looking for an alternative to a CD or a treasury bond and don't need the liquidity.

A few years ago the insurance companies developed a strategy that is based on the fixed or guaranteed annuity platform but offers an opportunity for a better return because it is linked to some type of index. Called a **fixed indexed annuity**, it follows a particular index, most commonly the S&P 500. However, over the last several years I have seen many insurance companies add multiple index strategies within their contracts so you have a variety of indices to choose from. As with any kind of an annuity contract—or any kind of an investment for

87

that matter—you need to look at these with caution to see if these strategies do in fact fit your needs, whether they will provide you with the types of guarantees that you want, and whether you can deal with the restrictions that exist in some cases.

When you're dealing with a fixed indexed annuity, you're given an opportunity to get a part of the gain of that particular index. You won't get 100 percent of the gains, but you will never have any of the losses. If the market goes up, you have a gain up to some type of a limit. If the market goes down, you stay the same. You never lose interest or principal unless you take money out of it. For that reason, I call it "Steady Eddy." You lock in a gain and you protect your principal. It goes up, it doesn't go down, and it truly compounds.

Remember what happens in the stock market? You have a gain but then it turns around and drops, so you just lost those gains. In order for you to compound your money, you have to get back to that high point and then go above it. With an indexed annuity, you never lose the gains, and so you add to those gains as soon as the market goes back up. Even if the market drops by 30 percent, as soon as it starts going back up, you're going to participate in those gains. Although you're limited on the upside, you eliminate the downside. You protect the principal, you protect the gains, and you truly compound your money.

A fixed indexed annuity won't give you 100 percent of the market gains, but it won't give you any of the market losses. Think of it this way. Suppose we're driving down I-75, heading to Florida. We're going 80 miles an hour. We pass a truck that's doing about 65. We get several miles ahead of that truck. Then we decide to stop, take a break for a few minutes, and go to a rest area. Maybe we'll grab a quick bite to eat, (like a $2 bag of chips or perhaps an overpriced candy bar). Anyway, we take about 15 or 20 minutes before we get back to the car and hit the road again. Soon we're up to about 80 miles an hour again and we're flying down the road.

While we were taking a break, the truck has continuously been going at 65 miles an hour. It caught up to where we got off, passed us, and went several miles ahead of us. Now, how many miles do you think we will go before we catch that truck again? (No, this isn't one of those weird math problems; it's just an analogy). It's going to be a long time before we catch that truck. Hopefully we won't have to pull over again. But unfortunately little Johnny drank too much pop and you know what happens next. We pull over again, so now it will take us even longer to catch that truck. That's how your indexed annuity works: it's the truck. You're not going to be going as fast as the stock market on the upside, but you're never going to have to pull over. It will steadily climb, steadily return your money, and steadily grow your money without ever going backwards.

This is a strategy that goes back again to our basic question: Is it more important for your money to grow, or for it not to shrink? Is it more important to get a steady rate of return and a constant compound or to get a big hit and then deal with a big loss? Then get another big hit, and maybe deal with another loss down the road? The uncertainty of the stock market can be replaced with the certainty of a "Steady Eddy" return, if you're willing to accept the fact that your returns are somewhat limited, and the accessibility of your money is somewhat limited as well. In many cases, when your portfolio is properly set up, these types of annuities can be a very good, solid core base to your portfolio, especially for a future income plan, one that will guarantee your standard of living and make sure that you will always have income while never having to worry about losses to the stock market.

A Last Word on Annuities

As I said at the beginning of this chapter, there is a lot of information out there on annuities. Some of it is very favorable, some is less favorable, and some is what I consider to be unbiased. I look for the facts, the sources that eliminate both myths and misconceptions. It is certainly true that annuities have been abused by certain advisors. With any annuity, as with any kind of investment, it's critical to really understand how—or if—it meets your needs. What are the pros and cons? Understand that all annuities—variable, fixed, or indexed—limit your access to your money. They all offer some kind of free withdrawal, which varies from company to company. As I stated earlier, this is most commonly 10 percent. In addition to this free withdrawal, most companies offer additional free withdrawals if the owner needs to take out funds for health care, hospital stays, or death. Taking out more than the free withdrawal triggers a penalty on the excess amount. This is called a surrender charge. You need to be aware of what the surrender charges are, but I have found that if the annuity is set up properly as part of an overall retirement plan, surrender charges rarely come into play.

There is no perfect investment. We always have to look at the good and the bad.

With an annuity, it's no different. Suze Orman has written a lot of books on personal finances and financial freedom. In her book, *The Road to Wealth*, she discusses annuities and gives a very good explanation of the differences between fixed, indexed, and variable annuities. She points out that indexed annuities are usually better in a bear market rather than a bull market. In a bear market the market is going down, and that's where these really shine, because they don't go down. When the market goes up, you start locking in gains where you left off, not having to recover any losses. In a bull market indexed annuities aren't going to perform as well. They're going to go up continuously, but they're not going to go as high. The market will certainly outperform them in a bull market, but indexed annuities will typically outperform the market far and away in a bear market.[6]

Another book I can recommend is *All About Annuities: Safe Investment Haven for High-Profit Returns* by Gordon K. Williamson. He goes into great detail on the advantages of annuity investments and the reserve requirements on the insurance companies, which are very impressive.

"A bank has to have about 17 cents on hand for every dollar it takes in, but an insurance company has to have a dollar in reserve for every dollar that it has taken in. Those reserves are regulated. During the Great Depression, it wasn't the U.S. government that bailed out the banking industry; it was the U.S. insurance companies. When we take a look at the history of these companies for guaranteed types of contracts, they have a strong history of providing safe returns in all kinds of economies."[7] Although they aren't perfect they are worth considering; look at them with caution, of course. Be sure to get the facts, and avoid the myths and misconceptions that are associated with these things.

As I said earlier, I understand that there are many myths out there about annuities. I talk to people all the time, and I'm almost afraid to use the words annuity in my meetings. Because as soon as those words come out of my mouth, I can see the hair on the back of people's necks standing up. And that is understandable, because annuities have been abused. I remember one couple in particular, whom we'll call George and Liz. We were talking about where they were going to be drawing their income from and the different sources that they had. They told me they were concerned that if the market went down again as it did in 2008, it would greatly affect their income. And that was true. It would cause them some serious sleepless nights.

I said, "Well, at this point in your life, would you say that it is more important for you to have a sure thing for your income or a possibility? In other words, would you say you'd rather have a sure thing for your future income?" They said, "Absolutely." So I said, "Well, that probably means that the best way to guarantee your future income from your portfolio is to use some type of annuity. What do you feel about that?" Immediately they said, "We hate annuities." I said, "Okay. Why do you hate them?" George said, "Well, because they're loaded with fees. My brother in-law lost a bunch of money when he had one." I said, "Well, it sounds like he had a variable annuity."

I explained that variable annuities go up and down with the stock market. I told them that there are different types of annuities and that if they should look at one that would provide them with a steady rate of return that would go up but not go down when the market goes down, it might fit their income needs quite well. I said, "What we should do is look at what amount of income it can provide. Then we'll look at the pros and the cons of it, and cut through all the myths. Let's get right to the facts: the good, the bad, and the ugly."

George and Liz agreed with that, so we set up a follow-up meeting to review my recommendations for them. I recommended using a fixed indexed annuity for a portion of their assets. It would provide them with a really good income for the rest of their lives. I explained the trade-off, that they would not have 100 percent access to those monies. There was a 10 percent withdrawal feature. But we would not want to touch these monies until it was time to pull income. The longer we waited to pull income the greater their income stream would be.

Chapter 7. Protect Your Core Income

We would want to set them aside and not worry about them. We would use the monies that they had in other assets for their liquidity needs, making sure they had plenty of emergency funds, and making sure that they still had money to grow, that they wouldn't have to worry about drawing income from. When we looked at the numbers, a fixed indexed annuity fit their needs very well. Once we discussed all of the aspects of the annuities in more detail, George and Liz decided that the fixed indexed annuity was indeed a good option for a portion of their assets.

Don't just make a decision based on what you've heard, or what you've read, or what somebody told you about annuities. Take a look at them yourself. Look at the different types of annuities and see which ones might best fit your needs, if any. Make your decision based on facts, not on myths or misconceptions. Make a good decision based on facts, not emotion.

As an independent advisor, I have the ability to give people a very broad view of different kinds of annuities and different companies, without having to be loyal to any one company. My loyalties are always to my clients. As I mentioned in the introduction to this book, it's also my responsibility as a fiduciary. Remember: when you're trying to set up your retirement umbrella and protect your future standard of living, you always have to go back to our basic question. Is it more important for money to grow, or for it not to shrink?

If you want to make certain your future income will be there, then there are only a few investment vehicles that can give you this kind of certainty. That usually points back to a fixed or guaranteed annuity. It can be a key piece of your retirement umbrella, one that will protect your future standard of living, allow you to sleep well at night, and greatly reduce your worries about your future income.

Chapter 8.
Myths, Misconceptions, and Misinformation

When it comes to planning for your retirement, you can find all kinds of advice. Some of it is good advice, some of it is bad advice, and some of it is just plain wrong. There are an awful lot of myths out there and people seem too willing to believe them. In this chapter, we'll take a look at some of the most common myths and misperceptions.

Why are people so drawn to all these myths? It occurred to me that it's really like the stories you hear about trying to lose weight—all the different diet tips that are out there. I can relate to that.

Over the last 20-some years, my weight has gone up and down. I've never gone into extreme obesity, but I've been pretty heavy. I always tell people losing weight is easy; I've lost thousands of pounds.

Obviously, the problem is keeping it off.

There are so many different diets out there, and the problem is that they are often very radical. You lose weight very quickly, but it's easy to put the weight back on as soon as you're off that diet.

For instance, there's the Adkins diet. Many, many people have lost thousands of pounds on the Adkins diet, which basically eliminates carbs, so no bread, no pizza. Well, I'm a pizza-eating machine. I love pizza. If you take me off of pizza, I can handle it for a while, but I'm going to go back to it. The problem with the Adkins diet is that as soon as you go back on the carbs, you gain a lot of the weight back.

Another popular option is a vegan diet. Going vegan will help you shed weight fast. But most people are meat eaters. When you go vegan, you eliminate meat completely. Even eggs are a no-no. You're taking anything with a face out of your diet. You're even eliminating milk. You use things like rice milk instead.

It's a drastic change, and it's almost impossible for most people to maintain it, because it's such a dramatic difference from what you were raised eating, what you were used to eating, and what you've been eating. In many cases people go right back to eating their steak and eggs and hamburgers, and as soon as they start adding those things back to their diet, their weight often balloons right back up to where it was.

The reason many diets fail is that they are way too dramatic. They require way too much of a change.

Chapter 8. Myths, Misconceptions, and Misinformation

It's hard to eliminate what we love. For example, I love meat. I love steak; I love a good juicy hamburger. It's easier for me to back off on portions than to just eliminate those foods completely. I found that when I started eating better food combinations, the weight started to drop. Once it dropped, I found it much easier to maintain my weight. I was still satisfying my taste buds with the food that I liked. I simply just ate a better combination of foods, and less of them, instead of just gorging myself on a gargantuan pizza. I would try to make my pizza day Friday, and I wouldn't eat it any other day. I would try to make my steak day one day of the week, and instead of a big old baked potato drenched in butter and all the other goodies on it, I would get rid of the baked potato, and use broccoli. Broccoli is a complex carb that helps break down the proteins. By doing those simple types of things, I found it a lot easier to lose weight, and maintain that weight loss, than I did with any of those radical diets that would take the weight off more quickly.

By now you're probably wondering how all this applies to planning your retirement income. Here's how: Radical diets appeal to us because they give us quick results. We're emotionally attached to those quick results. And when you take a look at the emotion that we see in the stock market, it's the same thing. It's the quick hit, the quick fix, the quick gains, that are so attractive to us. We want our money to go up 30 percent. We love it when we see a statement that shows our balance has gone way up. That quick fix is almost addictive. The problem is, as quickly as it can go up, it can go down. Just like the radical diet, where we get that quick fix and gratification, the quick hit in the market doesn't give us long-term protection. It doesn't offer that long-term steadiness that we can count on. We need to focus our investments and our strategies on getting that steady return, and avoiding the emotion that goes with those quick hits, and those quick big returns that can easily go back down.

So let's turn our attention to the title of this chapter, Myths, Misconceptions and Misinformation. The financial world is just loaded with all of these. Many of them are based on emotion. We have an emotional attachment to our success, but falling prey to the most common myths can actually destroy that success. Let's look at what I call the five most common retirement myths, one by one.

The Five Biggest Myths

Myth #1: Buy and Hold

The first myth is, buy and hold always wins. But buy-and-hold, or what I like to refer to as "buy-and-forget," doesn't always win. As a matter of fact, in the 2000s, buy-and-hold has been a disaster. In the '90s,

Chapter 8. Myths, Misconceptions, and Misinformation

buy-and-hold worked incredibly well. You were a genius. Everyone was a genius. If you had a *Wall Street Journal* and a dart, you picked the winners. It really seemed to be that simple. The market went up, and it just continued to climb. We had very few market blips in the '90s, and those that we did have, we recovered from very quickly. So when the 2000s come along, people had the same mentality, expecting the market to just keep climbing.

When the market did start to drop, right out of the chute, most people weren't concerned, because they just expected it to come right back up. But it didn't. It went down in 2000; it went down in 2001; it went down in 2002; and then it finally started to come back up. It finally started to break even somewhere around February of 2007. It went a little bit higher, and then we hit the crash of 2008. It took several more years to get that back. So buy-and-hold, during the first thirteen years of the new millennium, did nothing but get back what you lost.

The problem with the buy-and-hold mentality is that you are not compounding your returns until you get back to the high point and go continuously above it. If it goes back down, you're going to lose some of your returns. So that's the first myth. You have to be careful with buy-and-hold. Remember what we said in Chapter 5: The only way to protect and lock in a gain in the stock market is to sell. And that's something which is very difficult for most people to do, because we're emotionally attached to the possibility of quick return.

Let me tell you, your advisor also has a hard time telling you when to sell, because he or she may be afraid that they're going to tell you to sell at the wrong time. If they tell you to sell and the stock keeps going up, they look foolish. If they tell you to sell when it's down it's almost like admitting that they gave you bad advice in the first place. You can see the difficulty, and why buy-and-hold remains so popular in this industry.

Myth #2: Big Returns Require Big Risks

The next myth is that you can't make big returns without taking big risks. This goes right back to my diet analogy. We're always looking for that big hit, that big thing that'll drive our gains up, just as with our weight, where we're looking for the magic diet will drive our weight right down. In both cases we're looking for those big hits. We're told in the industry, and in all the financial publications we read, and on all those financial shows on CNBC, that you can't make big returns without taking big risks: "You've got to be willing to take risk." "How much risk are you willing to take?" "In order to get a good return, you have to take more risk." and so forth.

Chapter 8. Myths, Misconceptions, and Misinformation

I don't buy that. I think that you can get a good return without taking so much risk. As a matter of fact, by using the right strategies, you can greatly reduce a lot of stock market risk. This allows you to compound your returns by not having to recover as large of a loss. By locking in gains and protecting principal from time to time, you truly compound your returns. Don't take as much risk and don't be afraid to sell some of those assets when they do well.

Myth #3: Average Returns Tell the Story

You'll hear this one often: "The average return tells us an accurate story." Well, I'm here to tell you that an average return, folks, is not exactly what you think it is. Imagine this: You invest $100,000, and in the first year, you get 100 percent return on that money. Your $100,000 grows to $200,000. Wow! Don't we all love that? Well, the next year, all of a sudden you have a 50 percent loss, and your $200,000 is now back to $100,000 again. All right, you're still breaking even. The next year, boom, there's another 100 percent gain and you're back up to $200,000. You're all excited; but, lo and behold, another 50 percent loss comes along, and you're back where you started, with $100,000.

What was your average return over those four years? Do the math: Your average return was 25 percent, but what was your real return? How much did you lock in every year? You didn't lock any of it in. You

103

started with $100,000 and that's what you have today, so your average return is 25 percent but your real return is zero. What do you think about that?

Myth #4: You Can Do It Yourself

This is another myth that I hear a lot. I'm not saying that you can't do it yourself. I'm saying that you should be cautious and be aware of the different factors that affect your financial decisions. All too often I run into people who make decisions based on emotion, or they look at past performance, as we explored in a previous chapter. They make decisions based on wrong information or on the emotion of wanting to get those big hits. There's nothing wrong with trying to do these things yourself, but you need to use some tools. You need to look very closely at how your investment choices will perform in various markets. Don't just pick investments based on emotions. Choose strategies based on facts. You can find are a lot of excellent resources, especially online. You can look at fees, expense ratios, drawdown, and a huge amount of technical data. But don't get caught up in all the numbers. Choose wisely based on your needs.

An advisor's role is to help take the emotion out of managing your investment portfolio. They should help you make good, sound decisions based on facts—not on their opinion. Be careful if you find you're dealing with an advisor who is so opinionated and so affiliated with a specific type of strategy that they don't look at anything else. If your advisor is focused on one particular strategy, and is very negative towards alternative methods, then I would be careful. They may be limited in what they can offer based on the firm that they work for. It might even have something to do with how they get paid. Be careful about who is giving you advice and what their real motivation may be.

Myth #5: If It Were That Good, Everyone Would Be Doing It

This is another one I hear frequently: If something is that good, everyone would be doing it. Well, I don't necessarily agree. It's one of the side effects of all the misinformation that's out there. Given the prevalence of various myths and misperceptions, people have the wrong information, and it leads them to bad decisions. They're not making sound decisions based on facts, maybe because they believe some of the untruths that are out there.

Here's a case in point: I met with a lady a few months back. We'll call her Karen. She had a variable annuity. We did some research on it, then called the insurance company and got all the facts together. When we found out how much her fees were, what the return had been over the many years she'd held it, and what her income payout would be, it was without a doubt not what she thought. The performance had been far less than she thought it was. The future income Karen was hoping to receive from that annuity was going to be substantially less than what she had assumed it would be—what she had been told it was going to be—and it was not going to do what she needed it to do.

The problem was that she was enamored with her advisor. She just did not want to believe that person would have ever put her into something like that. She felt like I wasn't telling her the truth instead of accepting the fact that her advisor hadn't really put her into a very good strategy at all. She was more willing to believe the lie than the truth.

Unfortunately, that's something I see all too often. Sometimes the non-truth sounds better than the truth. What you really want is the better return, the bigger gain, and the greater income. But the fact is, you may find that your strategies are not going to provide those. You have to ignore the myths, get the facts, and eliminate the emotion.

And the Myths Just Keep On Coming...

How do these myths get spread around? I'm amazed at how many people listen to some of these radio and television personalities who are very popular, and they just take what these personalities say as gospel. People are sure that something must to be true because it came out of the mouth of somebody who is famous all over the United States. In reality, many of these radio personalities are not even licensed advisors. They simply give their opinions, and often the opinions they give are just designed to draw a bigger audience. They're getting paid to get ratings, not to give good advice. What does that do? Well, it's all about drawing that bigger audience. You will often find that the advice they offer is really not as accurate as what you might expect it to be. You really need to look at how it applies to your individual situation.

You often hear myths about mutual funds. A study by the financial services research firm DALBAR showed that the real rates of return on most mutual funds were nowhere near what people thought them to be.[8] In many cases the returns were substantially less than what the actual stock market indexes would have provided over the same period of time at a much cheaper rate. Remember this: With a mutual fund you're paying a fund manager to buy and sell stocks in the hopes that they'll perform better than what the index does, but the reality is that most of the growth mutual funds underperform the stock market itself. Internal fees inside of the funds have a lot to do with that.

Remember what we said earlier about mutual fund performance. In the '90s, everybody did really well;

but that has not been the case in the 2000s. Many of these mutual fund managers lost 40 to 50 percent of their money twice during the first eight years of the new millennium. Don't make the mistake of choosing these investments based on the opinion of some radio personality. Be sure you've really looked at the facts and cut through the misinformation that's out there.

Another area that generates a lot of myths is annuities. We dealt extensively with annuities in Chapter 7, but I want to touch on them again here. I understand that many people are afraid of annuities precisely because they have been fed so much misinformation about them. Here are some of the myths that we hear all the time. One is, "If I die, the insurance company keeps all my money." That's actually true of the "life option only" payout, but that is a payout that I would almost never recommend. It's rare that we would ever use that type of a payout, though in the right circumstances it could make sense.

Most of the time, when you choose some type of payout, you're going to choose a period certain. In other words, if you chose a 10-year certain or a 20-year certain, that means that the payment will come to you or your heirs for that period of time no matter what. If you chose a life option payout, the payout will end at your life. When you are using an annuitized payout, which most people don't do, you must be aware of the terms of the payout.

The fact is, if you die with a deferred annuity contract, whatever is left in that contract goes directly to your heirs and avoids probate. In most cases there are no fees or surrender charges taken out. There are a few exceptions, which you will know about up front before you enter into that contract, but in almost every case 100 percent of that money goes directly to your heirs.

Another annuity myth is that there is a lot of risk to your principal. That's true of a variable annuity but it's not true of a fixed or indexed annuity. The risk in a variable annuity is that your investments will go up or will go down with the market, depending on what the investments are. Any mutual fund will go up or down with the market. A fixed or indexed annuity, goes up but does not go down.

The third annuity myth is that annuities are loaded with fees. That's true for many, though not all, variable annuities. The vast majority of variable annuities are loaded with different types of fees. You have to be aware of what those fees are, how much they are, and how they benefit you. What are you getting for your fees? They offer a benefit, and it's just a matter of determining whether that benefit will actually benefit you. That's what you need to find out. What is the benefit and is it worth the cost for that benefit? Variable annuities can have some very high fees associated with them. Indexed and fixed annuities, however, do not have fees associated with the standard contracts.

Now that you know the truth, you can dispel some of the myths and have much greater certainty as you seek to protect your standard of living. Just get the facts.

With any investment, you always want to get the facts. Remember the old TV show *Dragnet*? Think of Joe Friday's famous line: "Just the facts, ma'am." When you have the facts, you're going to be able to avoid the myths, misconceptions and misinformation that trip up so many people. You'll be able to make good, sound decisions, put your retirement umbrella in place, and protect your standard of living for the rest of your life.

Chapter 9.
Your Retirement Take-Home Pay

Let's say that you've done a really good job of saving and investing your money. You've put your retirement umbrella in place and you've done it wisely, choosing your investment strategies and retirement savings vehicles based on the facts, not on myths and misconceptions. Now you're ready to draw income. This is what you've worked your whole life to achieve, to reach retirement so that you can live more comfortably and not be tied to the hustle and bustle of getting to work every day. Now it's time to enjoy the rewards of your hard work and wise planning.

Now your take-home pay will be coming not from your employer but from your retirement income. Let's look at how we make sure that your take-home pay in retirement will be what you need it to be, for as long as you need it. Remember that our goal is to protect your standard of living for the rest of your life. How much do you need to do that? How long will your money last?

We've touched several times in this book on the four income streams in retirement. Remember that there are only four, and for some readers, there may be only one or two. These are the four income streams: 1) your Social Security Income; 2) your pension if you have one; 3) continued work, whether full-time, part-time, or consulting; and 4) your own savings and investments. Those are your four options. If you don't want to work in retirement, you're down to three, and if you don't get a pension, you're down to two. So how long will your money last?

If you're down to two income streams, they are Social Security and your own assets. You can begin to draw Social Security at age 62, but for every year that you can delay Social Security from age 62 to your full retirement age, your payment will increase by six and a quarter percent plus the cost of living adjustments, if there are any. So sometimes it makes sense to delay Social Security, even if it means tapping into your own assets; other times it doesn't. We have to look at what's right for you and your needs.

The bottom line is that we can't just look at the income that you can generate from your savings and investments. We have to look at the take-home pay from that income. Just as when you were working, when you made $1,000 in a week, you didn't take home $1,000. After taxes and all the other things that come out of your paycheck, what did you take home?

112

Chapter 9. Your Retirement Take-Home Pay

Well, it's the same way in retirement. When you take money out of an IRA, you have to pay taxes on it. And when you pay taxes on it, it's going to reduce the amount of money you're going to be taking home.

Whenever you take a look at how much you're going to need in retirement, you have to take into consideration the old bugaboos of taxes and inflation, because your income needs to keep up with both of those. How can we be sure that your take home pay is exactly what you need? Remember that in retirement, a dollar is not a dollar, and $50,000 is not $50,000. What it will be depends on what your tax bracket will be. We can't know exactly what your tax bracket will be in retirement, and my gut feeling is that tax brackets will be going up. I don't want to see that happen, but I think it's likely, given the amount of debt the country has.

The retirement take-home pay that will support your standard of living will be what you take home after all those taxes are considered. But you also have to account for inflation. When people get a pension, they normally receive a specific amount of money every month, but most pensions do not factor in inflation. They stay flat. I see very few pensions that have an inflation factor tied to them. What does that mean for you? Let's say your pension is $2,000 a month. Well, in 10 years $2,000 is not going to buy the same goods and services that it does today. In 20 years it's going to buy even less.

Think back to my examples of what we paid for a new car in the 60s, or in the 70s, or in the 80s. It was substantially less than we pay today. Everything goes up—and if your pension isn't keeping up with inflation, your money and your take-home pay are going backwards. What can you draw from that will guarantee that your income will keep up with inflation and taxes? This is where it becomes tricky. You need a strategy that will not only provide you with an income today and at the start of your retirement, but also continuously provide you with an income that will maintain your standard of living for the rest of your life. That means keeping up with the taxes and inflation, and having alternative sources to draw from or having a pension-like payout that will at least keep up with the basic consumer price index inflated prices.

Be careful when you calculate how much you're going to need. Always understand the fact that a dollar is not a dollar when you pull it out of an IRA.

Determining your take-home pay in retirement can be a tricky business. Let's look at how one couple did it.

Tom and Susan's Story

Not long ago, I sat down with a couple to discuss their pending retirement. Let's call them, Tom and

Chapter 9. Your Retirement Take-Home Pay

Susan. They were excited because they had worked for many, many years—both had worked at the same place for over 30 years. They had done well. They had saved a substantial amount of money and they were really looking forward to retiring at a fairly young age. Both of them were going to be in their early 60s. They were going to be too young at retirement to draw Social Security, and they weren't planning on turning it on at age 62. Remember that when you turn on Social Security earlier, you reduce the amount that you're going to get.

When I met with Tom and Susan and we factored out where they were going to get their retirement income, the one thing that surprised them was how much they would have to pull from their IRA to get the income that they needed. They had completely forgotten about taxes.

They figured, "Well, we need $3,000 a month, so we just pull $3,000 out of our IRA and we're all set." I had to tell them, "No, $3,000 is not going to give you $3,000, because you're going to have to pay taxes on that $3,000." When we worked through a CPA firm to account for all the factors of their deductions and taxes, we calculated that they would have to pull out about $4,500 a month to get the net $3,000 that they needed. They were pretty shocked. The good news is Tom and Susan had plenty of assets to be able to pull that kind of money out without running out of money.

The way we had set up their pension payout and their income from their assets was going to provide them with that $4,500 each month. The other factor we needed to account for was inflation. So when we set up an income we had to include increases to keep up to inflation. In their case we used an indexed annuity with an inflation benefit that increased their income yearly so they would get regular raises. This enabled them to maintain their standard of living without ever having to worry about running out of income. They were surprised at how much more they were going to have to pull out to get the net income that they were looking for, but the assets that they needed to accomplish that were there. Tom and Susan's story had a happy ending.

Not every couple is as fortunate. I had another couple in a similar situation, and when we talked about how much they would have to pull out of their retirement assets to supplement their Social Security, I found that they had not considered the tax factor. When we started looking at how much they would really have to pull out of their retirement assets to be able to meet their additional income needs, they found that they did not have enough money. They had plenty of money in their retirement assets if they didn't have to take taxes out, but since they have to pay taxes, their money was simply not going to last as long as they had thought. That was even before we considered inflation as a factor. Be careful when you're looking at your retirement take-home pay. What is your real take-home pay?

What If ...? When a Spouse Dies

When you are a married couple planning your retirement take-home pay, you also need to look at how your income is affected when one of you dies. If a husband and wife both get Social Security and one of them passes, the survivor loses the smaller benefit and keeps the larger one. Is one of your income streams a pension? Pensions are often set up with a default that provides the surviving spouse with half of what the pension recipient was getting. You can arrange to take a lower payout and ensure your spouse will get the same amount. I can tell you about that from personal experience; it's what my father did.

My father worked throughout his career as a high school guidance counselor. He never made a lot of money in the '60s and '70s; those positions didn't pay much back then. When he retired in the mid-'80s, he retired with a really good pension, and he also got Social Security. My dad decided to delay Social security until he was 70 so that he would get a larger payout. He also decided to arrange his pension so that if he died, my mother would receive 100 percent of what he received. That way if he passed away, my mom's income would hardly change at all. Lo and behold, he died at the age of 72, shortly after he retired.

My mom, who is now—at the writing of this book— age 92 and very healthy, has lived way beyond her life expectancy. Her standard of living has been quite comfortable because her total income from my dad's pension and Social Security is roughly double what she really needs to live on. She has more spendable income now than my parents ever did when we were kids growing up. How can that be? The reason is that my dad made sure that my mom's income would be protected if something happened to him.

I can't tell you how often I run into couples who don't prepare for the "What if?" scenario. I have to ask them, "What if one of you passes away? What will happen to your income if you do pass away? When we take a look at Social Security, you're going to lose the smaller benefit. When we take a look at pension, there's a high probability that your benefits are going to drop way off." Again, you have a choice at the time you start your pension, and that decision needs to be considered very thoroughly. It could even cause your spouse to go back to work at an older age. What are you going to do to protect your income for the rest of <u>both</u> of your lives? Planning your retirement take-home pay as a couple is certainly important, but you also have to ask, what happens to your take-home pay if you die early or your spouse dies early?

Chapter 9. Your Retirement Take-Home Pay

In many cases, a death can cause a dramatic reduction in income that leaves the surviving spouse in a poor financial state. The simple moral of the story here is this: Understand what is going to protect your standard of living for the rest of both of your lives, not just one of you. Make sure you understand what will happen when one of you passes.

Whenever I meet with clients I always like to do what I call a "Booming Income Report." The report shows you where you're going to be getting your income from in retirement. Remember our four possible income sources: Social Security, pension, continued work, and your own retirement assets. In the Booming Income Report, we put them all in line, side by side, so that we can see how much you're getting from each of them. Then I take one of the spouses out of the picture—usually the husband, since women generally outlive men. I'll say something like, "Now, let's take a look at what would happen to our income if Mr. Smith dies at the age of 72." It can be quite dramatic.

I did this just a few weeks ago with a couple we will call Mark and Carol. When we looked at their Booming Income Report they were both very much concerned. If Mark were to pass away, the amount of Social Security that Carol would lose was going to be pretty dramatic, because her Social Security was almost as large as his. His Social Security was over

$2,500 a month, but hers was $2,400. Remember, when one of you passes, you lose the smaller benefit. In this case, that would be almost half of the family's Social Security income.

In addition, Mark's pension was going to drop to half. Carol would only receive 50 percent of his pension. So if Mark were to pass away first, the household income would change dramatically, in their case it changed by more than $35,000 a year. If Carol passed away first, Mark's income would drop by about $28,000 a year because he would still get his full pension. These are the possibilities you need to consider. How would you fill that additional income gap if something like that were to happen?

I don't want to be morbid, but in marriage there is a high probability that one of you may live much longer than the other. If you are a husband and wife in your early 60s now, there's a good chance that one of you may to make it into your 90s. Whether it's you or your spouse, what happens to the income when one of you passes? How are you going to fill any additional gap?

Chapter 10.
Long-Term Health Care

In setting up your retirement umbrella, it's important to be thorough. We need to look at all of the possible scenarios. That means we need to consider the possibility that someone in your family will need long-term health care.

This is a topic that is near and dear to my heart because I can speak from personal experience. My mother-in-law has been in a nursing home now for three years with severe Alzheimer's. Unfortunately, as the population continues to age we're going to see more and more of these care facilities. Many of them are already full to capacity with long waiting lists.

The nursing home where my mother-in-law now resides originally had an eight-month waiting list. We were fortunate to be able to get her in there sooner than that. If you want to get a bed in a nice nursing home, you find they fill up quickly.

I'm not going to give you advice with this chapter. I'm not going to tell you this is what you absolutely need to do. I do want to make it clear that you should be talking to a professional about this to help guide you through the process. You need to make sure that you're doing things correctly, because doing them incorrectly could result in thousands of dollars in lost income. I won't go into detail here but I can certainly direct you to available resources.

I will tell you this: If you have a loved one who is in need of additional care, the good news is that there are a lot of really good programs available. Your loved one may qualify for some assistance through one of those programs—for instance, the Veteran's Administrative Pension Benefit, which is for veterans and spouses of veterans who served during a war. He or she may qualify for an additional income that will help pay for at-home care, assisted living or nursing care, even if the at-home caregiver is a son or a daughter.

You may have heard horror stories about people going broke in order to get nursing care in relationship to Medicaid. That doesn't have to be the case. There are resources available to help. It's important to work with a good elder law attorney. I've worked on many such elder law cases with attorneys in Michigan as well as in Kentucky and Ohio. Their expertise is invaluable in helping people find a good nursing home and pay for it without going broke. Todd Schmitz, owner and founder of the Elder & Disability Law Firm in Mount Clemens, Michigan, has written numerous publications on this subject; you can find a list on his website, www.mymacombplan.com. I've done a lot of work with Todd and his team to help people get good care and qualify for Medicaid without having to go broke. But the process can be complex and stressful if you don't have good advice. Even when everything is done correctly, there are a lot of steps that have to be done in order to qualify.

So if you are looking at the prospect of getting a loved one into a nursing home and you want to know how to qualify for Medicaid without you or your loved one having to go completely broke, you should be talking to an elder law attorney who specializes in doing just that. You can go to the American Academy of Estate Planning Attorneys website (www.aaepa.com). There's usually an attorney in every state who can help you guide you through the process in a very professional manner.

Obviously, there are other options that would be better than having to hire an attorney and go through the process of trying to qualify for Medicaid, which does restrict the type of place you can go to. Insurance, for example, would be an option to be able to pay for that care without having to use your own money.

Speaking from Experience

As I said earlier, I speak from my own personal experience on this topic. When my wife and I realized that my mother-in-law was going to need additional care, we started to search for a really nice facility that would be able to take care of her. It was obvious that her care needs far and away exceeded our abilities to help her as well as my father-in-law's abilities to help her. Getting her into a care facility was essential. That started our search.

Once we found a place that we thought met her needs and was very nice, we discovered that the expense was excessive. At the time of her admission, the cost of her stay there was just under $9,000 per month. That sounds ridiculous—and it is—but understand that it is not abnormal. We're seeing fees like that all over the place as the cost of care continues to climb higher and higher. If the average cost of care continues to climb at the rate it has over the last several years, it is very likely we will see the cost of care at a professional nursing care facility exceed $15,000 per month within the next few years. That is devastating to somebody's savings. Unless they're very wealthy, most people are going to get wiped out pretty quickly.

We talked in a previous chapter about the fact that people are living longer. One of the reasons is that we have good health care. People who suffer from diseases that once were considered fatal are now able to be treated and their life expectancy is being extended. So how do we pay for health care as we age?

Paying for Care: What are the Choices?

With careful planning you can make sure you're able to pay for long-term care. Let's talk about some of your options.

Pay for care out of your own pocket. This is the most direct option, but how fast will your money be depleted if you have to start paying $8,000, $9,000, or $10,000 per month for nursing care? What will that do to your portfolio? Remember, even if your loved one is able to stay at home, he or she will still have expenses for at-home care that can exceed $3,000–5,000 per month.

Purchase long-term care insurance. This can be a good option but you need to understand that it can be difficult to qualify for long-term care insurance, more so that other types of insurance. Remember that insurance companies have many years of experience with life insurance claims. As the population ages and people live longer, the cost of life insurance is actually going down. But in many cases, the reason people are living longer is that they are getting care somewhere. If they're in a care facility they may live a long time, but the cost of their care at a facility could be excessive.

All of that means that insurance companies have been raising their rates on long-term care insurance premiums. In fact, most long-term care insurance policies do not have a guaranteed premium. Most companies will only guarantee their premium for two years; at the end of those two years they have the ability to raise your premium, sometimes dramatically.

Several years ago one of my clients called me. Let's call him Ray. He was 85 at the time, and he said, "Kevin, I just got my long-term care premium notice and it's gone up 92 percent." I wish I could tell you that was uncommon. I told him that premiums were starting to go up because the cost of care was going up. Insurance companies are allowed to do that as long as they raise it on across the board for a specific age group. They can't raise it for only a particular client.

Ray asked me what he should do. I was honest with him. I said, "Well, if I tell you to discontinue the premium, I could be giving you some horrible advice. If you have to go into a nursing home, you could start spending thousands of dollars every month for your care. On the other hand, you might never use that insurance." We looked at it realistically. I suggested we call the insurance company and see what his options were. We found out that if he removed the inflation benefit from his policy, his premium cost would stay about the same. That would still give him some coverage to provide for his or his wife's needs if either of them went into a nursing home, but they wouldn't have to worry

Chapter 10. Long-Term Health Care

about the premium going up for the next several years. Our other options were to lower the amount of coverage or to just get rid of the policy altogether.

When you make decisions like this you also have to consider your age and your spouse's age. Now once again, I don't want to be morbid, but in reality, if you go into a nursing home in your mid-80s you're probably not going to be there a long time. On the other hand, if you go into the nursing home at age 70, there's a high probability that you will be there a long time.

Going back to our example, Ray and I decided that his best option would be to lower or remove his inflation rider so that his premiums would stay the same but he would still have some pretty decent coverage. Lo and behold, within a short period of his making that decision, his wife had to go into a nursing care facility. It's a very good thing that Ray kept that policy because it's been helping to pay for her care. Without it her care would have cost him many thousands of dollars every single month.

You've got to be careful. Long-term care insurance can be a great benefit for people, but you have to understand what the moving parts are. Can your premiums go up? What are the factors involved in that? Can you buy a policy that you can pay up in 10 years or 20 years and then be done with it? That might be an option.

Purchase a hybrid insurance policy. Because long-term care insurance policies are so expensive, are hard to get, and have no guaranteed premiums, they have become pretty unpopular. Because of that, insurance companies have developed an alternative. Many insurance companies now offer a life insurance policy that has a three-way benefit. The benefits are: 1) a cash value, which means the money is accessible to use for whatever purpose you'd like; 2) a death benefit, which means that if you die, 100 percent of the money goes to your beneficiaries and is tax-free to your heirs; and 3) a living benefit that allows you to draw some, if not all, of the death benefit, to use for nursing care, home health care, or assisted living.

These policies vary from company to company so you want to be careful. Be sure to get the facts. Basically, it offers you an alternative to just buying long-term care insurance. These policies will give you a benefit somewhere down the road. Either you will use the cash value and get back most, if not, all of the money that you put into it, you will have a death benefit from which your heirs will benefit tax free, or you will use that money for living benefits for home health care, assisted living, or nursing care. Those hybrid types of policies can be very popular.

There is another version of this idea which is an annuity into which you deposit money. It's a tax deferred annuity contract that pays a guaranteed interest rate. It's very safe. It's not going to give you a gargantuan rate of return. It's going to be just whatever the fixed interest rates are paying, probably somewhere around two percent as of the writing of this book. But it will grow. It will also offer a benefit that will in some cases double—if not more than double—the actual initial deposit if you take it out for nursing care costs or assisted living. Those policies are not as popular as the life insurance version but there's no underwriting involved at all. It's strictly the amount of money you put in and then they give you a bonus or an additional benefit on top of what you deposited to use for assisted living or nursing care.

Many life insurance or annuity contracts offer a payout that will double if you need the money for assisted living or nursing care. If you were drawing an income from an annuity that had that type of benefit attached to it, your benefit would double. If you were getting $2,000 a month for income, it would double to $4,000 a month if you needed it for nursing care. Beware of the fact that these benefits come with some requirements. Perhaps the benefit can only be triggered after the income schedule has been started for a period of time—which might be 1 or 2 years. Always check to see what will allow you to trigger the additional income benefit.

These are some of the options that are available, and you should look at them carefully to see if any of them fit your needs. The cost of care can really wipe people out very quickly. We all hope it will never happen to us, but in all honesty, long-term care needs will affect about one out of every three people over the age of 65 in some way, according to the statistics I've seen.[9] It's a horrible thing to have happen and if you are not prepared it can be devastating, not just emotionally but also financially. The best advice I can give in this area is to be careful and be prepared.

Chapter 11.
Fees, Fees, and More Fees

In the world of finance, there is no shortage of fees. I refer to them as money slipping through the cracks. They are fees you may not even know you're paying. They're everywhere, and we see them in a variety of different ways. Some of them are right out front where we can see them clearly. One example would be a brokerage fee that is taken out of your account every quarter. You'll see that on your statement. Another would be a fee paid when you buy into a mutual fund. That may be a percentage taken off the top before you go into the fund. Again, that's a fee and you'll see it right away.

The obvious fees are one thing, and you can easily account for them in your planning. The danger and the unexpected expense lie in the many fees that are hidden from view. You may not even know you're being charged these fees, and believe me, they can be excessive. One of the more common financial products that is often loaded with fees is a variable annuity. This is not to bad-mouth variable annuities. I'm not a big fan of them but they do have their place.

The fees exist for various reasons and there are benefits that those fees can offer. But as with anything else, you need to look carefully at them. What fees are you being charged and what are you getting for those fees?

A variable annuity may carry a mortality and expense fee. It will have what we call subaccount fees. It may have rider fees. It's not uncommon for these fees to be in excess of 2.5% to 3.5%. They may be even higher, depending on the company. I have seen fees as high as 4 to 5 percent per year. In most cases, these are fees you don't even know exist. You don't necessarily see them being subtracted from your account. If you have a rider or additional benefit added to your account, then you will usually see those fees. But the other fees are not subtracted from your account—they simply reduce the return. They're just part of it. It's important to understand how much is it costing you to have this account and what is it providing. What are you paying for? The prospectus will show everything except the transactional cost inside the separate accounts. Since separate accounts are very similar to mutual funds I will refer you to the explanation of those fees below in the mutual fund fee section.

Brokerage accounts are also loaded with fees in many cases. These sometimes come in the form of transitional costs where you have to pay a fee when you buy and/or sell a security. There might be a commission to buy or sell. There might be a fee inside of the fund itself. In some cases, mutual funds have not just management fees but also 12B1 fees. There may be other types of fees inside of the mutual fund, that are part of the fund itself, and that you don't even know about.

Hide and Seek: Spotting the Hidden Fees

Where do you find information about all these hidden fees? Keep in mind that most of the mutual fund fees are in the prospectus that you receive—and that most people don't read.

You know the document I mean. I call it a nap waiting to happen. It's that big thick document that everyone gets whenever they buy a mutual fund. It's always in fine print that you can barely read without Mr. Magoo-style magnifying glasses, and most people don't bother to read it.

Along with the fees that are disclosed inside of the prospectus, every mutual fund also has what are called transitional costs. Those are the costs for buying and selling the stocks and bonds inside of all mutual funds. That's right. Inside of your mutual fund, your fund manager buys and sells stocks and bonds on a regular basis depending on the objective of the fund manager or managers. In many cases, if you have multiple mutual funds, you have different fund managers who are buying and selling securities throughout the year. As they buy and sell there are cost involved to make those transactions and you are paying to buy and sell stocks and bonds that you didn't even know you owned. Those fees are called transitional costs.

Why aren't those transitional costs included in the prospectus? The mutual fund companies don't show those costs because while the prospectus will tell you what the fees will be going forward for the management, the advertisement, etc., they don't yet know how much buying and selling they will do over the course of that year. So how do you get information on transitional costs? If you call the fund company and ask specifically for the fund's Statement of Additional Information, they will make that statement available to you. The statement of additional information goes back over the past year and it will tell you what it cost you to buy and sell inside of that mutual fund.

These fees can be quite shocking, and you have to be aware of them in your planning. You'll also find fees associated with insurance. Many life insurance policies—especially universal life and variable universal life insurance policies—have fees associated with them. These fees can apply not just to the insurance costs, but also for the underlying investments themselves. Sometimes it's a management fee; sometimes it's some kind of processing fee. With any asset, you always need to find out what it is costing you to own that particular type of asset. You may need to dig a little deep to find that out, because sometimes these fees are not just right in front of your face. I have a process I use to help people better understand the fees associated with their accounts.

That brings me to a story. Several months ago, a lady came into my office and we sat down to discuss her portfolio. She had several variable annuities and several mutual funds. We took one of her variable annuity statements and called the company. We asked them a series of questions, which I had all laid out for her, to find out exactly what the internal cost of that variable annuity was. In her case, we discovered that she had a mortality and expense fee of 1.5 percent. She had an average management fee of 1.2 percent. She had a rider fee of 1 percent. That totals up to 3.7 percent. That means that in order for her to just break even on her investment, it has to improve by 3.7 percent. If it goes up 10 percent, her real return will be only 6.3 percent. Understand those fees are the ones you can easily see. They do not include the transitional fees.

I recommend a book called *Does Your Broker Owe You Money?* by Daniel Solin. In one chapter, he offers behind-the-scenes tidbits of what goes on inside of the investment world. He discusses how people invest, the fees that are associated with investing, the different techniques used by brokers, and so on. It's interesting and eye-opening. It can be almost scary in some ways, to understand the true cost of owning mutual funds or what you really need to understand before you get into something.[10]

Here's the bottom line. No matter what investment you have—stocks, bonds, mutual funds, variable annuities, life insurance, etc.—there's usually some kind of internal cost or fee involved in owning that asset, not just the cost of what you put into it. What does it cost you to own that? I'm a firm believer in understanding what those costs are, what those fees are, what you're getting for those fees, and whether they meet your needs. I always put the costs into actual dollar amounts instead of percentages, because seeing the dollars involved makes it more real for the client.

In my view this is another key piece of planning and putting your retirement umbrella in place. You always want to do a breakdown of the type of assets that you have and ask the right questions from the holders of these funds so that you can get a clear picture. Does this meet your needs? Will it help to protect your standard of living, or will it just be an unnecessary cost? In my experience, digging into the basic cost of some assets, especially things like variable annuities and high-expense mutual funds, will give you information that will help you make much better decisions about your investments and provide increased protection for your standard of living. Take the time to understand your hidden costs. You'll be glad you did.

The Retirement Umbrella

Chapter 12.
The Basics of Life
Insurance

The subject of life insurance could fill an entire book by itself. I'm not going to discuss it in detail here, but I don't want to overlook it, because one of the questions I hear most frequently is, "How much life insurance should I have?" And my standard answer is, "It depends." That's a great answer, isn't it? It's the truth. Your choice of life insurance depends on what you want to provide to your loved ones.

Let me use myself as an example. At the writing of this book, I'm still working; my youngest child is 10 years old. If something were to happen to me, he would need income for a long time to maintain his standard of living. So my wife and I want plenty of life insurance to be able to replace my income, provide for his future education, and cover other needs. If I am still around when he gets older, our need for insurance will not be as great. By the time the kids are out of the house and have their own families, we will not necessarily have as much need to replace my income. The kids will need insurance, but my own need for insurance may diminish. On the other hand, I might desire insurance in order to pass on a legacy to my family. My need for insurance changes. My desire to be able to pass money on is not necessarily a need; it's more of what we call a legacy gift. Once everybody's out of the house, I may want to have life insurance so they get tax-free benefits when I pass away.

Years ago I had a client who told me that he kept buying more life insurance because he wanted to pass on tax-free money to his kids. He said, "I'm going to spend my money. My kids will get life insurance, which is better for them anyway, because that's tax-free, whereas my IRA would be totally taxable." He plans on spending his money, but he's using some of his money to buy life insurance to be able to pass on to his kids.

The need for insurance varies from family to family and person to person. The type of insurance that is best for you really depends on what your needs are. There are two basic types of life insurance: term life insurance and permanent life insurance. There are many different types of permanent insurance, and even combination plans using both term and permanent together.

Term Life

People who are working and would need to replace their income need a lot of insurance, and the cost of insurance can be very expensive. In most cases, when you are trying to get a large sum of life insurance for a period of time—say a 10-year or 20-year period—the best option is to "rent" it, or buy term. That's exactly what **term life insurance** is; it's renting insurance for a period of time. At the end of that term, the 10- or 20-year period, the cost of insurance will go way up, or the insured may simply have to drop it altogether. You'll hear many radio hosts out there telling people, "Buy term and invest the difference." That may or may not work, depending on your need and desire for passing on a legacy to your family beyond that period of time, because once the term is up, your cost for insurance could go way, way up. With most (but not all) term policies there is no cash value.

Permanent Insurance

Permanent insurance comes in basically two forms, but a *lot* of different combinations and choices: **whole life** and **universal life**. **Whole life insurance** is one of the oldest types of insurance in existence. It's been around for hundreds of years.

Whole life insurance is guaranteed for the rest of your life as long as there's money in the policy and you've been paying premiums. In most case the premiums are going to be much higher for the same death benefit then you would get with term insurance, but in most cases, the policy will produce interest and maybe dividends that at some point might be large enough to pay the premiums internally.

For a very long-term insurance need, you may want a permanent policy in place. Whole life might be a good option for you, as long as you understand that the premium cost is substantially higher. You may even choose a whole life/term life combination, or a policy that covers two people but only pays a death benefit on the second death. Those types of policies are typically used in estate planning, or to provide money for a special needs child or dependent. There are some other benefits that life insurance can provide, such as income if the cash value is large enough and that income can be very tax efficient. That is a much deeper and more advanced discussion that we won't go into in this chapter. For the basic death benefit, whole life insurance is typically the most expensive type of insurance in the short term, though it may actually prove to be cheaper in the long term.

Chapter 12. The Basics of Life Insurance

That brings us to the other type of permanent insurance, which is called **universal life**. Understand that this type of insurance does have some internal costs that need to be considered. These fees and expenses will have a big effect on how long these policies will go before they run out of money and lapse. So again, look at *all* the facts, but here are the basics. There are three types of universal life, fixed, indexed and variable. **Fixed universal life** or UL pays a fixed interest rate of return on the cash value. **Indexed universal life**, or IUL as it is often called, is very similar. However, instead of only giving the owner a fixed interest rate of return the return will actually be linked to how a particular index moves. If the index goes up, you have a gain on the cash value; if the index goes down, you have not gained on the cash value. **Variable universal life** is linked to some kind of a subaccount, like mutual funds, that will go up or down with the market. You've got to be careful with a variable universal life policy, because you could lose money in your investments, and that could cause a problem with being able to pay for the insurance. Again, caution is required here.

Both of those types of policies offer flexibility that may allow you to increase or decrease the premiums, but if you decrease them, you have to be careful. If you don't have enough money in that policy in your later years, it could cause the policy to lapse. With a universal life policy, the cost of insurance does not stay level as it does with whole life insurance; instead the cost increases. The older you get, the more expensive it gets. If you have a universal life policy, whether it's a fixed universal life, indexed universal or variable universal life, you really need to have it reviewed to make sure that that policy will last all the way through the rest of your life.

Many years ago I worked for a company where I did administrative reviews for these types of policies. I found that many of them were going to lapse about the time the clients reached the age of 85. Understand that if the policy lapses, these individuals will have no death benefit left. There is no death benefit, because they have run out of money. So be careful. There are fees inside of these accounts, costs of insurance—and they can eat up the policy if you don't keep it funded. You don't want to get a letter from the insurance company that says, "Hey, if you don't put more money into this thing, you're going to lose it." In some cases, that might even cause a taxation—which could be a big disadvantage.

In the end, I want you to understand that there are different types of insurance, and you need to determine which is best for <u>you</u>, depending on <u>your</u> needs. Just because someone tells you, "Don't ever buy anything but term life, or you're an idiot," doesn't make it true. In many cases, if you're using insurance for a long period of time, permanent insurance might make more sense. Remember what we said in Chapter 11 about long-term care. Sometimes you can get a permanent insurance policy that has more than one type of benefit. In addition to a death benefit, you may have a benefit that offers assisted living, home health care, and nursing care costs as well. It's important to understand what your options are. Even more importantly, if you have a life insurance policy, and you haven't had it reviewed, I highly recommend that you have somebody do what's called an "in force" review to make sure your policy is going to do exactly what you want it to do, for the period of time you want it to do that.

Here's the last word on life insurance: there are other types of insurance, along with other reasons to have insurance—business, family protection, family disability benefits, and many more. I'm not going to discuss those here, except to reiterate that the choices you make about insurance are another important component of your overall retirement umbrella. Insurance plays a significant role in protecting your—and your family's—standard of living and providing a legacy. **Get the facts!**

The Retirement Umbrella

Chapter 13.
Questions and More Questions

One thing I've learned from all my years in this business is that there is never a shortage of questions: questions that <u>have</u> been asked, and even more questions that <u>should</u> be asked. I often find that people don't know what questions to ask, so in this chapter I want to help you better understand what you need to ask. I'll provide you with some specific questions for different situations—questions that will help you determine if what you're considering is, in fact, the right investment for you.

Throughout this book, we've talked about the importance of basing financial decisions on facts rather than emotion. I want to help you make good decisions based on logic and not on emotion. When we look clearly at the facts and apply them, we make good, clean, solid decisions that fit our needs. When we make decisions based on emotion, we often find the result doesn't fit our real needs because the emotion got in the way. We've covered a lot of ground in this book, and after reading this far, you probably have some questions. I hope this will help you better understand what questions to ask.

Mark Matson, who is an investment advisor and author, wrote the following in his book, *The Dirty Filthy Lies My Broker Taught Me and 101 Truths About Money & Investing*: "If you know the right things, you don't have to know everything."[11] I think that's true. You don't have to know everything. You need to know what applies to your own individual needs. I don't care how it applies to your brother-in-law, your sister-in-law, or your friends. It needs to apply to you. Too many people make decisions based on what they've heard from this person or that person who says, "Oh, I'll never buy a mutual fund," or "I'll never buy a stock," or "I'll never buy an annuity." They may have reasons for their decisions, but their circumstances may not apply to you.

In your situation, one of these things might be the right decision. You don't have to know everything; you just need to know the right things. I see too many people get into what I call "analysis paralysis." They start trying to analyze every last detail and then they can't even make a decision because they're overanalyzing. They think that they need to know every little micro detail. This is what you really need to know: the pros and cons, the good and bad, how this applies to your situation, and how it might improve your situation. Based on that information, then you can decide whether it makes sense for you.

What Do You Need to Know?

Let's take a look at some questions that will help you to know the right things. We'll start with what I call the Retirement Quiz. This will give you some good questions to ask yourself.

Retirement Quiz

Taxation Review

I have never heard of "phantom income."
True / False

I did not pay our CPA a "tax forward" planning fee last year.
True / False

I pay taxes on our Social Security income.
True / False

I report interest income, dividends or capital gains on page 1 of my tax return.
True / False

Income Review

I know what my core income need is.
True / False

I have never considered the effect that the death of my spouse will have on our income.
True / False

Our income is not guaranteed for the rest of both of our lives.
True / False

I have never thought about the most tax-efficient way to draw income in retirement.
True / False

I never really considered factoring inflation for my retirement income.
True / False

I do not have long-term health care insurance.
True / False

I have never considered or discussed the alternatives to long term care insurance.
True / False

Risk vs. Return Analysis

I own mutual funds.
True / False

I have never heard of the term "drawdown."
True / False

I have never been shown the overlap in my current investment strategies.
True / False

Chapter 13. Questions and More Questions

I have never looked at the internal cost of my current investments.
True / False

I do not know what the real return of my portfolio has been over the last 10 to 15 years.
True / False

I do not have a plan for getting out of the market when or if it falls.
True / False

I am not using the advice of a fiduciary when making investment decisions.
True / False

Financial Decision Making

This book has taught me at least two concepts that I did not know.
True / False

I have likely made decisions based on myths, misconceptions or incorrect facts.
True / False

I do not have a written process for making financial decisions.
True / False

If you—and your spouse, if you are married—answered true to more than two or three of these statements, that's a clear indication that you really need to sit down with someone who can help give you good solid answers.

When I meet with people, I always start with this retirement quiz. I also ask them whether they own a variable annuity. As we discussed in Chapter 7, there are a lot of possible pitfalls and hidden fees associated with variable annuities. If you own a variable annuity, or you are considering purchasing a variable annuity, you should be able to answer these questions.

Variable Annuity Questions

Company name: _____

Policy: _____

Issue date: _____

Surrender value: _____

Accumulation Value: _____

Death Benefit Value: _____

Chapter 13. Questions and More Questions

Death Benefit Lock in: _____

Income rider value: _____

Income rider payout ratio: _____

What is the roll-up rate on the income benefit?
_____

How does the income rider affect the death benefit?
Pro Rata or Dollar for Dollar? _____

Other Riders: _____

Policy Guarantees: _____

Variable Annuity Policy Fees: _____

Mortality and Expense Charges: _____

Management Fees: _____

Administration Fees: _____

Advisor Fees: _____

Rider(s) Fees: _____

12B1 Fees: _____

Sub-Account Fees: _____

Other Fees or Expenses: _____

Can any of these fees be dropped? _____

If you don't have the answers to these questions, you need to call the company that issued your variable annuity and insist that they provide you with this information. If they are unwilling to do that, you might want to replace that annuity or avoid that purchase.

Mutual Fund Fees

Understand that there are different types of mutual funds. Some require charges to get in or out of them; some have yearly fees, others do not. This will help you understand the inside cost.

Front End Load / sales charge: _____

Back End Load / sales charge: _____

Expense Ratio: _____

Management Fee: _____

12B1 Fee: _____

Transitional Cost: _____

The Liquidity Question

You can see that I ask a lot of questions of my clients and prospective clients. This is one that they always ask of me: How much liquidity do I need? It's an important question, and I often find that people misjudge the answer. Most people either have way too much liquidity or not enough. Neither situation is good. If you have inadequate liquidity and are hit with an unexpected expense, all of a sudden you need to remove money from an investment. You may lose money to a removal fee transaction cost; you may also lose money if you are forced to sell during a market downturn. If you have liquid monies available, then you can take the money from that source and not have to worry about it. That's good.

On the other hand, I see people quite often—especially senior seniors, who have been retired 10 years or more—who seem to think that they need large amounts of liquidity, sometimes in excess of five or six years' worth of their actual expenses. How much liquidity do you really need? You need to consider what that liquidity is costing you in what we call the time value of money. Could you get a better return if you put it into a CD? Liquidity is great, but don't overdo it with money that's in a very low-interest-bearing account.

In most cases, the penalty for getting out of a CD is just a couple months of interest, which means that if you put money in the CD and then two or three months later you needed to pull that money out, you're going to get hit with an interest penalty. But it is interest that you wouldn't have earned in the first place if you had just put the money into a bank account. Don't be afraid to use CDs for some of your liquidity needs. They can be another key piece of your retirement umbrella.

The Retirement Umbrella

Chapter 14.
It's Never Too Late

We've covered a lot of ground in this book. We've looked at retirement fears and risks and myths. We've looked at common retirement vehicles and at various strategies that can help protect your standard of living. All of these things go toward putting your retirement umbrella in place, so you can sleep well at night without worrying about your retirement income.

Now I want to leave you with one last story, and one last piece of advice.

One day a few years ago I came home from work. As I looked around, it occurred to me that I should mow my lawn, but it was a beautiful sunny day, and I just wanted to enjoy the sunshine. We live on some property out in the country, so mowing the lawn is not a small job. I have about four acres to mow. It's not a quick 10-minute mow job. It takes a while. Sometimes it's nice to get on that mower, put the earphones on, and just sit back and mow away, but that day I didn't feel like doing it. It was a nice day and I felt like doing some other stuff. Mowing the lawn didn't really seem to be a priority. The weather was nice and I knew my schedule for the week was pretty light, so I figured I could take care of the lawn the next day or the day after that. It was no big deal.

I decided to just kick back and do something else. The next morning, the weather was beautiful, and predicted to remain good. So I was going to mow the lawn later and enjoy the day, but later, the winds picked up and an unexpected storm blew in, which resulted in rain for the next five days. As you can probably imagine, by the time the sun finally did come out, the lawn—which was already pretty high when the rain started—had grown excessively thick. I jumped on the mower and started mowing away. And wouldn't you know it? Something broke on my lawn mower before I mowed even a tenth of the lawn.

That put my lawn mower in the shop, which of course meant that while it was in the shop, my grass was growing, and growing, and growing. By the time I got the lawn mower back from the shop, my grass was so incredibly high and thick that I had to mow it four times just get it back down to normal again. And that's not all. By the time I finished mowing, there was so much dead grass that I even had to rake up about two acres by hand. Believe me, that's not a job that you want to do, especially in the heat of the summer, but it had to be done.

Chapter 14. It's Never Too Late

I'm sure you can guess the moral of the story: Don't procrastinate. If I had taken care of the lawn in the first place, I wouldn't have had that problem. I might even have avoided the lawn mower repair.

Procrastination is so easy and so tempting. It's something that we all want to do. We tell ourselves, whatever the task is, that it doesn't have to be done today. We can always do it tomorrow. But then tomorrow comes and we tell ourselves the same thing again. We do it over and over again; we do it with lots of different things. I know that right now as you're reading this, you can think of something that you've put off repeatedly until you can't put it off any longer. Whatever that might be, now it's going to take much longer, and maybe even be much more expensive, for you to do it.

When it comes to your retirement umbrella, procrastination is one of the biggest risks you face. It's a big old storm that threatens to just blow the whole umbrella wide open. You have to take precautions in your retirement planning to avoid the risks that may arise. You can't afford to procrastinate. Your retirement umbrella can protect your standard of living for the rest of your life and your spouse's life, but you have to put that plan in place. That means anticipating the risks we described in this book and preparing for them, because you can't foresee everything that will happen. There are always surprises. I recommend a book called *But*

What if I Live? The American Retirement Crisis, written by Gregory Salsbury. All too often, he says, the problem is that the things that we never plan on are the things that happen and the things that can cause us some serious issues.[12]

If you prepare properly for the "what if" scenarios, and understand what your choices are, then the things that do come up are not as devastating as they could be. Avoid procrastination. Set up your retirement umbrella to protect against these unforeseen events. As we've discussed in this book, understand the four sources of retirement income, understand your fees, and understand where you will be pulling income from in your retirement. If some of these financial storms come along, how might they affect your future standard of living?

Procrastination can be a big risk, but the good news is that it's not too late. It's never too late to get started, whether you're 30 years old or 85. There's always something that can be done to help you avoid financial storms. I've worked with people in all types of age groups. Some make the excuse that they're too young; others tell me they're too old. They're both wrong. Their needs will be different and their plans will be different, but there is always something they can do. An 85-year-old widow is probably going to be more concerned with making sure that her estate will pass on in a very efficient way, that it will avoid probate, that it will minimize taxes to her heirs, and that it will provide her legacy. A 50-year-old couple will more likely be concerned with making sure that their retirement income will be there when they're ready to retire in 10 or 15 years, that they will be able to grow their money, and that they will have an income to provide them with their established standard of living for the rest of their lives. The couple has plenty of time to accomplish what they want to accomplish prior to retiring. The widow has already been in retirement for many years but it's not too late to provide for what's important to her, which is making sure that her estate is in proper order. These are two completely different sets of concerns but each has time to take care of those concerns. It's not too late for them, and it's not too late for you. **Start today**.

The Retirement Umbrella

About the Author

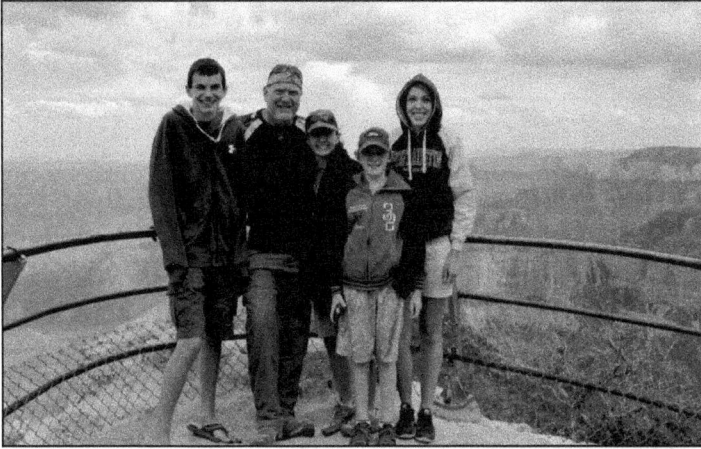

Kevin Bard is the owner and founder of Creative Asset Solutions, LLC. He is respected financial consultant, educator, and author. Kevin is also a retirement and social security specialist who focuses on maximizing income solutions and protecting investment principal. His strategies have helped his clients preserve their wealth and increase their family legacy.

Kevin is a series 65 investment advisor representative and holds firm to his fiduciary responsibilities; in addition, he holds life and health insurance licenses in multiple states. Kevin is a longstanding member of the Society of Financial

Service Professionals, and both the Cincinnati Area and the Eastern Michigan Better Business Bureau, maintaining an A+ rating since starting Creative Asset Solutions, LLC in August of 2001. Kevin's firm is based in Northern Kentucky, with branch offices in Cincinnati, Blue Ash, West Chester, and in Clinton Township, MI.

About the Author

Kevin Bard
Creative Asset Solutions
kevin@creativeassetsolutions.com
www.creativeassetsolutions.com

Michigan Office
18645 Canal Rd., Suite 2
Clinton Township, MI 48038
Phone: 586-228-1282
Fax: 859-818-0409

Kentucky Office
7310 Turfway Rd., Suite 550
Florence, KY 41042
Phone: 859-372-6727
Fax: 859-818-0409

Ohio Office (Blue Ash)
4555 Lake Forest Drive, Suite 650
Cincinnati, OH 45249
Phone: 859-372-6727
Fax: 859-818-0409

The Retirement Umbrella:
Protect Your Standard of Living
and Enjoy Peace of Mind in Retirement

ISBN-10: 0-9883878-6-7
ISBN-13: 978-0-9883878-6-7

—Disclaimer—

Kevin is an Investment Advisor Representative with Bridgeriver Advisors, LLC, which is a separate company from Creative Asset Solutions, LLC. Past performance does not guarantee any future performance. Any guarantees mentioned are backed by the claims paying ability of the insurance company. CDs are FDIC insured, annuities are not. Before acting on any idea in this book please consult a financial, insurance or tax professional.

Although the author and publisher have made every effort to ensure that the information in this book was correct at press time, the author and publisher do not assume and hereby disclaim any liability to any party for any loss, damage, or disruption caused by errors or omissions, whether such errors or omissions result from negligence, accident, or any other cause.

Expert Press

References

[1] Colby, Sandra L. and Jennifer M. Ortman, Projections of the Size and Composition of the U.S. Population: 2014 to 2060, Current Population Reports, P25-1143, U.S. Census Bureau, Washington, DC, 2014.

[2] Colby, Sandra L. and Jennifer M. Ortman. The Baby Boom Cohort in the United States: 2012 to 2060. Current Population Reports, P25-1141. U.S. Census Bureau, Washington, DC. 2014

[3] Heimlich, Russell. "Baby Boomers Retire." *Pewresearch.org*. Pew Research Center, 29 Dec. 2010. Web. 22 July 2016.

[4] Scranton, David J., and M. G. Crisci. *Financial Insanity: How to Keep Wall Street's Cancer from Spreading to Your Portfolio*. Carlsbad, CA: Orca, 2011. Print.

[5] Cussen, Mark P. "Introduction To Annuities: The History Of Annuities." *Investopedia*. Investopedia, LLC, 12 July 2009. Web. 22 July 2016.

[6] Orman, Suze. *The Road to Wealth: A Comprehensive Guide to Your Money: Everything You Need to Know in Good and Bad Times: Revised and Updated*. New York, NY: Riverhead, 2010. Print.

[7] Williamson, Gordon K. *All about Annuities: Safe Investment Havens for High-profit Returns.* New York: J. Wiley, 1993. Print.

[8] Hanlon, Sean. "Why The Average Investor's Investment Return Is So Low." *Forbes.* Forbes Magazine, 24 Apr. 2014. Web. 22 July 2016.

[9] "Who Needs Care?" *Longtermcare.gov.* Long-Term Care, n.d. Web. 22 July 2016.

[10] Solin, Daniel R. *Does Your Broker Owe You Money?* Bonita Springs, FL: Silver Cloud, 2004. Print.

[11] Matson, Mark E. *The Dirty, Filthy Lies My Broker Taught Me: And, 101 Truths about Money & Investing: Is Your Broker Lying to You?* Cincinnati, OH: McGriff Pub., 2004. Print.

[12] Salsbury, Gregory B. *But What If I Live? The American Retirement Crisis: A Retirement Guide for Baby Boomers.* Cincinnati, OH: National Underwriter, 2006. Print.